More Praise for Charles Davidson's Foster's Pie Pan

Rich with stories and reflections from decades in pulpit and classroom and in open spaces, each personal story in Foster's Pie Pan *offers reminders of truths we depend on and refreshing perspectives on those truths—about how healing comes in surprising ways, and how the well-worn paths of ordinary life lead, again and again, to holy ground. As they turn these pages, readers of every generation will find themselves invited home.*

—**Marilyn McEntyre**, professor, writing coach, author of *Caring for Words in a Culture of Lies* and *When Poets Pray*

These stories are powerfully engaging. Davidson is a gifted writer, causing the reader to want more. Each chapter is laced with wisdom as the sacred breaks through with depth and meaning. I was so moved by the book that I read each chapter several times. Davidson's questions engaged me in deeper exploration of every narrative. This is a good read for pastors, parishioners, therapists, and clients.

—**James Hyde**, retired director, Program of Ethics and Pastoral Care, Department of Psychiatry, University of Louisville School of Medicine

Dents and discoloration marring the surface and texture of an old tin plate suggest its usefulness and value to those through whose hands it has passed. Following the theme set forth in this opening metaphor, Charles Davidson has composed a set of variations that explore nuances of the presence of grace within the lives of people in which its influence is not readily apparent. Imaginative weaving and reflection take the reader beneath appearances for a glimpse of transcendence at play.

—**Louis Reed**, Presbyterian Psychological Services, Charlotte, NC

In this winsome, witty, and wise collection of reflections, Davidson crafts moments that point towards the possibilities of seeing and experiencing divine grace. Readers will relish these stories as opportunities to glimpse and savor insights that capture occasions of transformation in our lives.

—**Paul Galbreath**, Professor of Theology, Union Presbyterian Seminary, Charlotte, NC

Since the dawn of human consciousness, people have told stories to help them understand their lives and develop new ways of living. In this collection, Charles Davidson introduces us to the people and places that have shaped his life and made him into the insightful and caring person he is today. It is storytelling at its best.

—**Walter R. Smith**, honorably retired Presbyterian (USA) minister, author, and teacher

Davidson's rich and varied stories shimmer with grace and assurance, in recognition of the fact that what we hold in common is holy. There is depth here that evokes the reader's own memory of similar events and people.

—**Keith D. Herron**, United Church of Christ minister; adjunct professor, Central Baptist Theological Seminary; former moderator, Baptist Cooperative Fellowship; author of *Living a Narrative Life*

Foster's Pie Pan

Stories Of Grace Abounding
In A Fallen World

Charles Davidson

Parson's Porch Books

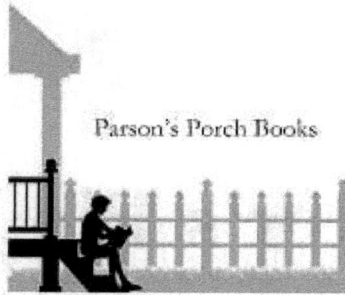

Foster's Pie Pan: Stories Of Grace Abounding In A Fallen World

ISBN: Softcover 978-1-960326-096

Parson's Porch Books is an imprint of Parson's Porch *&* Company (PP*&*C) in Cleveland, Tennessee. PP*&*C is a self-funded charity which earns money by publishing books of noted authors, representing all genres. Its face and voice is **David Russell Tullock** (dtullock@parsonsporch.com).

Parson's Porch *&* Company *turns books into bread & milk* by sharing its profits with the poor.

www.parsonsporch.com

Foster's Pie Pan

Dedication

For my beloved wife Georganne who with her discerning eye, listening ear, and constant friendship has put a song in my heart and a spring in my step during lakeside walks laced with smiles and laughter amid the stately poise of herons, the placid composure of turtles, the cheerful tweets of birds, and the eccentric chatter of ducks and geese.

Epigraph

"The mockingbird took a single step into the air and dropped. His wings were still folded against his sides as though he were singing from a limb and not falling, accelerating thirty-two feet per second per second, through empty air. Just a breath before he would have been dashed to the ground, he unfurled his wings with exact, deliberate care, revealing the broad bars of white, spread his elegant, white-banded tail, and sc floated onto the grass. I had just rounded a corner when his insouciant step caught my eye; there was no one else in sight. The fact of his free fall was like the old philosophical conundrum about the tree that falls in the forest. The answer must be, I think, that beauty and grace are performed whether or not we will or sense them. The least we can do is try to be there."

—Annie Dillard, *Pilgrim at Tinker Creek*, 8

Contents

Preface

The heart of this book is *story* about persons, seasons, occasions, and sacraments—human story and divine story intertwined and inseparable.

As my dear mother used to say, "A picture is worth a thousand words." The late George Buttrick was emphatic: "Simile, story, and symbol are far more effective carriers of truth than any syllogism . . . The Gospel comes through the power of parables."[1]

Consequently, this collection of writings, some previously published and others presented for the first time, are intended for anyone, laity or clergy, expressing a preference for *storied narrative* in contrast to the abstractions often characteristic of scientific, philosophical, and theological discourse.

Over the years as a pastor, teacher, and psychotherapist, I have written for the person in the pew and for the vocational practitioner. Biblical theology has been central to both endeavors, whether in Bible studies for the church school or in articles for ecclesiastical and professional journals. My biography of Vincent van Gogh addressed the general reader and the specialist since Vincent had something to say to each.[2] My edited volume of George Buttrick's lectures on preaching was offered to the preacher who must hold forth from the pulpit week after week, year in and year out, for the sake of the gospel and the worshipping community.

These pages take a different turn. They beckon us to a tobacco field next to a forest, the general medical ward of a

---

[1] Charles N. Davidson, Jr., editor, *George Buttrick's Guide to Preaching the Gospel* (Nashville: Abingdon, 2020), 87.
[2] Charles Davidson, *Bone Dead, and Rising: Vincent van Gogh and the Self before God* (Eugene, OR: Cascade Books, 2011).

mid-city hospital, a deep hole in the earth where shreds of paper lie next to fallen dreams and earthworms, a school where young minds come alive and others fall asleep, an artist's easel and a musician's piano, a fox's den and a chicken house, and your own ruminations during the process of listening in and observing.

Here you will meet an unforgettable person named Foster, and another named John, equally unforgettable, as well as "the incomparable Tooney."

You will encounter several generations of my grandparents and persons associated with them, including four African American slaves with whom I hope to commune in person when I die and go to heaven.

You will sit at the feet of a sea captain who was a parishioner in one of the congregations I served, whose memorial service I conducted. His high adventure on the midnight sea is one for history books and children's literature as well.

You will encounter Vincent van Gogh who needs no introduction. His life and art have touched more hearts than all the cardiac surgeons the world over.

You will rejoice in the presence of Beethoven and Mozart and let their muses ring in your ears.

You will enter the purple space of Advent, hearing "what I heard one morning in the sanctuary" and what I witnessed with my own eyes at age nine, marking a colossal divide of consciousness between the "before" and the "after." Then you will have a chance to consider the gifts you place under your Christmas tree as you get a snapshot of what hung on mine. Not least, you may ponder just what Christmas would mean if there were no Easter.

You will visit a backroads settlement in the Piedmont of rural Southside Virginia, where the foxhounds sniff and bay their way through the middle of the churchyard,

16

followed by hunters on horseback in white shirts, hunter-green jackets, brown breeches, field boots, and black velvet helmets; and where, as any well-trained preacher's dog would do, my yellow Lab, Buddy, with his snout to the air, yowls in tune with Sarah Adams' 1841 hymn, "Nearer, My God, to Thee," bellowing from the carillon beneath the steeple.

You will celebrate "A Day for True Love" with Saint Valentine as well as visit a retreat center in the beautiful mountains of western North Carolina for a "glimpse . . . of the treasure buried in all events."

Whether you consider yourself a dreamer or not, you can reflect upon the meaning of your own graduation day when in your youth you set foot into the adult world in response to your calling, to do a thing or two that may have seemed utterly preposterous at the time, and for which years later you remain grateful if uncertain as to what to make of it.

If you are curious as to what it's like to be a preacher coming up with sermon after sermon, Sunday after Sunday throughout the liturgical year, then "Some Wisdom from Woodchuck" may disabuse you of the illusion that it's by some magic formula, when more likely it's by the whisk of the wind whistling through the thorn tree, or the turn of a worm in the ground, that we preachers decide how to respond to "those outlandish things" that Jesus said about "God's unconditional grace."

You can leap from there to consider why "ministry is like sports" and "subject to the pointless competition of the steeplechase, the serious injuries of boxing (with shadows), and the deadly leisure of line drives aimed straight at the preacher."

Eventually, if you're up for it, you can accompany Saint Paul and his entourage of "established" Presbyterians, "aged like softened, cleanly sliced cuts of ripened Dunsyre blue

17

cheese ready for crumbling in Caesar's salad," as you advance together through an arduous journey toward the "screeching, screaming city of Ephesus with its ghettoes, ghouls, goblins, and gibberish" in the "interior regions" of Asia Minor, until you eventually arrive in the desert sands of Texas where under no circumstance would you invite yourself or your family for a summer vacation, unless possibly you live there. Then you must decide whether to stand still, stunned, demoralized, and arrested by inertia, or move your heart, hands, feet, and voice in response to what you have seen.

Lastly, along with me, you will find yourself recomposing your spirit and reengaging your calling on the tiny island of Iona off the west coast of Scotland "at the heart of a groaning creation, a 'thin place' in the eye of the tempest," where in the ancient greystone Abbey of Saint Columba you partake of the Holy Eucharist and give thanks for "always carrying in the body the death of Jesus, so that the life of Jesus may also be manifested" in you.

As you enter these pages and exit them, should "Grace" come knocking at your door, perhaps the posture you assume in readiness for further awakening to God's presence in your life was captured by Annie Dillard in a moment of rapt curiosity as she sat spellbound beside Tinker Creek.

"All I want to do," she said, "is stay awake, keep my head up, prop my eyes open, with toothpicks, with trees."[3]

What happens next awaits the sheer beauty and grace of the Spirit.

Charles Davidson
Asheville, North Carolina

---

[3] Annie Dillard, *Pilgrim at Tinker Creek* (New York: Harper's Magazine Press, 1974), 86.

PART ONE | Persons

1

Foster's Pie Pan

"They are all gone into the world of light,
    And I alone sit lingering here!
Their very memory is fair and bright,
    And my sad thoughts doth clear.

. . . .

O holy hope, and high humility,
    High as the heavens above!
These are your walks,
    and you have showed them me
To kindle my cold love."

—Henry Vaughan (1622–1695), "They Are All Gone into the World of Light"

HIGH ATOP A BOOKSHELF in my study sits a tarnished, weather-beaten tin pie pan that many a blue moon ago belonged to a man named Foster. He was a kind and gentle old fellow with a smudged face and scruffy beard. On his best days he appeared as tarnished and weather-beaten as his tin pie pan still does even now.

Bless her dear sweet heart, and despite the lovely and gracious person she was, my beloved and devoted maternal grandmother could never bring herself to let Foster cross the threshold into her home. His filthy and ragged attire was simply more than her cultured eyes could abide. The only realm in which she could "see to him," as she said, was that divinely appointed one where she believed as an article of faith that the shaggiest of poor whites were destined to dwell, which was beneath the scorching sun in communion with the hoe and in observance of the soil to which she summoned Foster for a hard day's work.

Foster wore a tattered dark brown felt hat with wide brim, holey at the edges, that stood above his meager world as a grand complement to the fact that only a few drops below the perspiration that hung from his furrowed brow he was missing most of his teeth. Without either knowing or in the least bit caring, Foster managed quite well to corrupt the King's English with every clause that whooshed and hissed from his tongue.

Foster's crusty countenance remains etched in my mind like a saint in a stained-glass window, for at the center of his universe he possessed the broadest, most glorious grin you ever saw on the face of a Cheshire cat.

Foster loved life. His enthusiasm for each day's splendor was his cardinal gift to the world. He also loved his Muriel cigars which were a coveted present from my grandfather.

Believe it or not—and I, for the life of me, would *not* believe it if I could—before Foster ever struck a match to light his newly acquired cigars, my southern born, southern bred, sexagenarian grandfather smoked those very same cigars first and foremost for himself. He did so down to an inch and a half of their life. Then, for what seemed an endless mile that fell far short of reaching an act of charity, he tossed the soggy cigar butts into a five-gallon drum. When the drum was full, he handed it to Foster. I know for certain because I saw with my very own eyes the unsightly exchange that took place between the two of them. What my grandfather got in return for his favor was ceaseless gratitude while Foster gummed the bitter remains.

As always, through his toothless grin, great laughter broke forth into the sunlight from the depths of Foster's soul. This was true in spite of the fact that, being as humble a man as I had ever seen, Foster spent his nights dwelling, literally and quite dismally, it seemed to me, within the confines of a chicken hut. There among the hens and roosters Foster made his feathered bed.

I remember my conversations with him and how glad he always seemed to see me, as on the occasion when I sat close beside him on the stone bench beneath the giant elm tree in my grandparents' back yard.

Truly, of all the cosmic sights I had taken in by the age of ten, few left a greater impact upon me than seeing Foster break his bread from that tarnished, weather-beaten tin pie pan. It is a memory that still clings to the pit of my stomach. The spectacle of his lifting to his lips the luscious food prepared by my grandmother was more than my tender years could comprehend. With my incredulous gaze glued to Foster's feeble frame, I wondered why on earth it was that he and I both partook of the same sumptuous delicacy yet never from the same dish. Mine was made of china, his of tin.

It was the intersection of those two discordant worlds, so near to one another and yet so far apart, situated as they were side by side for a finite moment under an infinite sky, that gave me my first glance of a third world coming to birth within myself. The potential for moral discernment took roots in my consciousness, as so often it does, in relation to another person whose worldly circumstance was diametrically unlike my own.

With eager delight and a thoroughly grateful look upon his face, Foster lifted his loaded fork to his mouth. And in that split second, at once intrigued and dumbfounded, I was transported into a realm beyond my imagining. For my wonder-struck eyes were suddenly transfixed by the portrait of a man, ancient and craggy and visibly thankful, holding as he was the food-laden pie pan in the palm of one hand as the juice of life ran down from the crevices of his mouth onto his whiskered chin, while with the other hand he sipped warmed-over coffee from a discarded Maxwell House coffee can.

It was Foster who with glee in his eyes taught me how to prepare a hill of dirt for planting potatoes, and, when their due season came, showed me how to dig them up full-grown with great care lest I mangle their delicate skin. I was to dredge the hoe, not hack with it. It became clear to me only considerably later in life that here was an early object lesson about how to bear oneself compassionately in the face of those tender situations in which people, like vulnerable potatoes waiting to be loosened from their sightless captivity, require acts of grace, not deeds of cruel and heartless rapacity.

Lo and behold, these many years later, too many to be counted and too precious few to be forgotten, I bear witness to what I believe was so uncommonly special about Foster, for all his earthly wretchedness and despite his every trouble and distress, surrounded as he was with pick hoes and chicken feathers, that permitted his spirit to be undaunted and his soul content. It was simply this: Did Jesus not say that as God's incarnation in the world he would come again and make his dwelling place among "the least of these"—"even as thou, Father, art in me . . . and I in them" (Matt 24:45, John 17:21–26, RSV)?

I can tell you for certain that in Foster's crusty, crumpled, and exuberant countenance I got my own unmistakable, first-hand glimpse of the face of Jesus. I am as sure of it as I am sure of anything. And ever since, this fact alone has made me a student of countless faces belonging to all sorts of unlikely people in all sorts of unlikely places.

When Foster departed his earthly abode, his world-weary flesh and bones lay on the floor of the chicken house with the roosters and hens cackling about him. Across his face, as wide and bright as the crescent moon against a solemn summer sky, shone that toothless Cheshire cat grin. It was the signature of a man who could neither read nor write, but who clothed in humility had obtained a glimpse into the very heart of God.

To ply beneath the surface, to catch a trace of the hidden riches that lie in the depths of the soul, is to see not only below the tarnished and weather-beaten image of every human creature. It is to meet living proof of the Creator God who resides deep down within each one of us. The measure of our true humanity consists not of the warts, blemishes, deficiencies, and craters of pain and misery that doggedly beset us. What defines our essence beneath this dense layer of smudge and stain is what dwells within us as the mysterious and everlasting Abundance, for which more than anything else we are thankful. For this grace is of far greater value than we ever dreamed, and of no less worth than the incomparable treasure revealed to us on any given day in the presence of angels like Foster.

"Even as thou, Father, art in me . . . and I in them."

Bless you and thank you, dear Foster. For, until I reach my own last horizon, I shall be unable to forget either the gleam in your stars or the crescent moon in your sky.

2

Grace Given as Grace Received

"I was a harness horse,
Constrained to travel weak or strong,
With orders from oppressing force,
Push along, push along.
I had no space of rest,
And took at forks the roughest prong,
Still by the cruel driver pressed,
Push along, push along."

—George Moses Horton (poet and slave, 1798–post 1867),
"Death of an Old Carriage Horse"

———————

STORIES HAVE BEEN PASSED DOWN about my
paternal grandfather Clarence, who died several years before
I was born, to the effect that he could take quickly to the
stern edge of his character and at times be brusque,
impatient, and demanding. While he was an industrious and
productive Virginia farmer who certainly knew the meaning
of hard work, with prosperous farmlands and fruit orchards
to show for it, he now and again failed to notice that others
worked equally as hard as he, and for far lower wages.

One such person was a long-time faithful farmhand by
the name of Elijah, who by this time had become an old
man, as had my grandfather. As always, the toil fell to Elijah
to till the ground. With his hand faithfully to the plow one
sultry summer afternoon, he struggled to keep his usual pace
behind the mule as from a distance my grandfather assumed
the inherited posture of one whose job it was to oversee.

It was common for Papa, as his children affectionately called him, and likewise for other white folks, to overlook the fact that the sweltering humidity had drawn beads of perspiration down Elijah's dark brown cheeks.

For a split instant as the mule turned in its path, the two old men stood side by side at the corner of the field.

"Mr. Davisson, would y' mine takin' holt of the plow whilst I go relieve myself?"

"Gladly, Elijah."

It not only had been ages since Grandfather had taken hold of anyone's plow, including his own, but for many years Elijah had accumulated a debt of more than just a few greenbacks that he still owed my grandfather. Circumstances being what they were during the Great Depression, coupled to the customary social, economic and political arrangement, such debt hung over Elijah's head like an iron cleaver. It precluded the chance that a poor and aged Black man would ever have hours enough in a lifetime, much less in a matter of months, to earn what it took to erase a debt that was part of a system of duties and obligations that kept one particular class of people subservient to another.

Elijah, a descendant of slaves, had spoken nothing of such obligations on this particular day; nor had my grandfather, a descendant of enslavers. Having obliged himself to do Elijah a small favor as the afternoon sun bore down upon the sweaty back of Elijah's trusty old mule, Grandfather took hold of the reins and plow handles as beneath the pummeling heat he jostled with the soil up one row and down the other. When Elijah eventually returned from his errand, Grandfather spoke the first word.

"You know, Elijah, it's been a long time since I've walked behind a plow. Mighty hard work, I'd forgotten just how."

"Yessuh, Missuh Davisson."

"Elijah, you know that $5,000 you currently owe?"

"Yessuh, Missuh Davisson."

"It's forgiven. You don't owe it anymore."

Elijah stood in sheer dumbfounded amazement, exclaiming, "Oh, thanks you, Missuh Davisson! Thanks you! Thanks you!"

A few months thereafter, early on a cold, blustery Sunday morn in January 1941, for reasons I have never fully known nor fully understood, concerning the extent of all that burdened him and made him a prisoner within himself, my grandfather Clarence went to the basement of his house and put a shotgun to his head and pulled the trigger.

The irony of what otherwise appeared to be a largely successful life, despite the share of human foible and failure to which all are entitled, was that Grandfather Clarence at age sixty-five, having forgiven the debt owed him by Elijah, for whatever reason could not forgive the "debt" he owed himself. Perhaps that, too, was in the form of a deficit long ago transmitted. My guess is that its effects had already begun to accumulate when at an early age he lost his mother to death's dark door. Being told that he was unmanageable, his father soon shuffled him off to live with a relative. The rage that more than once manifested outwardly eventually turned its way inwardly upon the self.

Sometimes it is necessary to invert Jesus' maxim, "As you wish that others would do to you, do so to them" (Luke 6:31, ESV), in order to say, "As others wish that you would do to them, do so to yourself."

Of all the besetting sins of an increasingly narcissistic age of emptiness and brokenness, the failure to love oneself may be a root sin that is perpetuated down the cycles of the generations.

In keeping with the Christlike virtue of losing oneself in order to love another, not to love oneself at all makes it virtually impossible to love someone else. "You shall love your neighbor as yourself," for only as grace is received can grace be given.

Grandfather in a graceful moment walked in Elijah's shoes. I do not know, nor can I know, precisely what that meant for my grandfather. Perhaps there dawned upon him the extent of personal sacrifice that Elijah had made for him for so many years, which in turn made it possible in a system that had wounded them both for the one to extend grace and the other to receive it.

Whatever may have been the case then, or soon thereafter upon that cold and blustery January morn in the basement of the house, I believe by the eternal mercies of Christ that Papa Clarence came at last, with Elijah, as shall we all, to receive the full measure of grace that shows itself upon the ever-loving face of God.

"Father, forgive us our debts as we forgive our debtors" (Matt 6:12, KJV).

3

The Slaves of My Ancestors

"It started that way: laughing children, dancing men, crying women and then it got mixed up. In the silence that followed, Baby Suggs, holy, offered up to them her great big heart . . . She told them that the only grace they could have was the grace they could imagine. That if they could not see it, they would not have it."

—Tony Morrison, *Beloved*, 88

DICK, STEPHEN, CHARITY, AND LUCY were their given names—these beloved "Negroes." They were the propertied slaves owned by my fourth great grandfather at the time of his death in the year 1810. At the top of the inventory of all of Philemon Davidson's worldly possessions, the court appraised Dick at 120 pounds sterling, Stephen at 100, Charity at 20, and Lucy at 90. Together they comprised more than half the pecuniary sum of the entire estate lumped together, down to and including five axes, a grindstone, two handsaws, a pair of spectacles, and one "woman saddle." It does not take a microscope to discern whose fingerprints fell upon the axe, the grindstone, and the handsaw.

Given the irrecoverable distance of the ancestral past from which these children of Africa had come into an unforeseen and splintered destiny in America, they and their fellow slaves passed through a myriad of predictable and unpredictable daily dangers to life and limb, including torture and lynching, as they trudged their beleaguered path toward the Promised Land.

From the vantage point of the auction block as slavery's narrow vista and constricted view of the future—"I'm here today and gone tomorrow"—these children of God were promised nothing remotely akin to a realized eschatology. Short of stumbling through the gates of heaven, theirs was a stumbling block into repeated disaster.

Shamefully and disgracefully, by legal decree if not divine dictate, due to the theological falsehoods of many preachers and the economic egotism of numerous slaveholders, the likes of Dick, Stephen, Charity, and Lucy were deemed, if not ultimately doomed, to the lot of mere mortal chattel. In an ethos of white supremacy wedded to the wealth of landed aristocracy and entitled gentry, this human "capital" was numbered among any "moveable . . . article of tangible property other than land, buildings, and other things annexed to the land."

In truth, every slave in the Old Dominion was affixed to an entire system of which the appurtenances included blistering hot rows of tobacco leaf baking beneath the scorching sun, outbuildings consisting of one-room shanties that housed and slept an entire slave family, and the bricks and mortar mixed with the sweat of the brow that built and sustained the Big House. Therein, the white master and missus partook of daily morsels of dough kneaded by Black mammies whose bruised feet stood atop packed earth while their gnarled fingers baked the loaves of the white man's freedom upon the iron griddles of oppression.

In that respect and with regard to the fate of the Black man, I lament the awful truth about one of my not so greatly esteemed ancestors. Opposite the branch of the family tree bearing my surname, there is a line that gave me my middle name, Nuckols. Philemon Davidson's great-great-grandson, my grandfather Clarence, married a dear and sweet woman,

31

my grandmother Susie Nuckols. Her paternal grandfather, Joseph Nuckols, being large of stature but small of heart, bore his strength in such a way that with his one hand held high in the air he lifted his slave man upside down by the feet, and with the knuckles of his other hand beat his slave man's rump into stinging raw meat.

Thus when the hopes and dreams of slaves sprang up like lilies in a scorched field, theirs were the songs and dances of a vision that, by faith, fashioned a cry: "O, come, sweet Jesus, deliver us!"

Nothing else, not anyone else except Jesus, sufficed to assuage the morning dread and curb the evening hunger. The underground rail to freedom for those who made it through thickets of woods to safe harbors hidden behind plaster walls and beneath knotty-pine floors was as turbulent as the waters of the Red Sea when God parted them for Moses to lead the Israelites out of Egypt. Only Jesus as Living Water could quench the thirst of souls whose bodies lay wilted in the heat of the noonday pestilence and whose spirits grew weary and faint from the hunt of the midnight rider.

Dreams and visions, not of an actualized fulfillment, but of imaginings with the scope of an unflinching mind's eye and pining heart's desire peering over the horizon, propelled these wayfarers to see beyond the brutal and bitter plague of their captivity. In a land flowing with milk and honey, the only true, wise, just, righteous, and loving divine Master of all would someday, on the far side of the Jordan, blessedly grant a better way of life than the crack of the whip and the curse of the hoe.

Think of it this way. Since none of us can see far down the line of vision, we can only trust past the point at which we do see. Dick, Stephen, Charity, and Lucy, plus countless others who endured the horrors of slavery in this unjust land, bequeathed us a gift of faith that defies the sight of an everyday imagination and ignites the power of an astonishing will to freedom.

To dream dreams and see visions, in life and death, is to dare to believe the impossible beyond the familiar. It is to picture that what has happened thus far along the way, some of it lovely and too much of it dreadful, simply cannot add up to the culmination of what life is about. To our world-fatigued eyes there is yet more to enter our line of vision than what has narrowed our vista and constricted our view. There is even far more of goodness itself still to come than, caged in the darkness, we can possibly imagine to be true.

Today, beloved children of Africa, you ache with the torment of fire in your bones, miserably attached to your shackles, hopelessly bound to your chains. Tomorrow—surprise!—in defiance of all that appears inexorable, you spring loose into the cool, fresh air of freedom. Your bruised feet and jagged toes leap from the soil with elation. Your scarred hands and crippled fingers touch the tips of the clouds in ecstasy. Your dry lungs and parched lips burst forth upon the firmament with praise. Halleluiah!

Dick, Stephen, Charity, and Lucy—this outlandish event called Resurrection is yours, not by chance but by Providence. Hooray for you as the last become first while the first become last! Seen through the eyes of your long-suffering faith as "the assurance of things hoped for, the conviction of things not seen" (Heb 11:1), this marvelous turnabout through God's everlasting grace and mercy is the one thing, the only saving thing, for a beleaguered soul to believe in.

To trust courageously against entire odds the line of vision your heart most desires, like the craving of sight by a blind person whose glass eyes eclipse the sun, is not so preposterous, after all, in the new Jerusalem.

"O, come, sweet Jesus, and deliver us!"

4

Sea Saga

"My soul is an enchanted boat,

Which, like a sleeping swan, doth float

Upon the silver waves of thy sweet singing;

And thine doth like an angel sit

Beside a helm conducting it . ."

—Percy Bysshe Shelley (1792–1822), "Prometheus Unbound," Act II, Asia

---

SHIPMATES, FRIENDS, AND FAMILY affectionately called him "Captain." Throughout his long years in the merchant marine, and until his dying day at the age of seventy-five, Thomas Cromwell spun many a captivating yarn, enthralling the hearts of young and old alike.

Sweltering in the summer heat of 1920, this proud sailor, in the prime of his youth, gambled his modest home and a small sum of cash as collateral against the purchase of a dream. He bargained for a seaworthy wooden schooner and commissioned himself as its captain.

Banking on the odds that goodness and justice eventually prevail against adversity and tribulation, he spent not so much as a dime on insurance. His only surety was the policy he had inherited from his parents, which was that sticking to his dream would see him through life's ups and downs.

With cargo, crew, and a few passengers aboard his newly acquired vessel, he set out upon the maiden journey of his lifelong odyssey at sea, with rights to trade in a certain commodity.

The captain's eyes scanned the glistening Caribbean waters that encircled the Cayman Islands from whence hailed his hearty clan of Gaelic descent. With his broad hands and gangly fingers protracting from his towering physique, he took hold of the ship's helm.

Possessing a natural disposition for a seafaring life, his ruddy complexion, sturdy countenance, and gentle spirit radiated a contagious smile that reassured all who looked to him to master the winds and waves of a sometimes wild and tempestuous sea.

It was toward evening at the sunset of Cromwell's inaugural day as pilot of his ship that he descended below deck to retire until daybreak for some well-deserved rest. Freed from focusing upon the ship's compass or a distant object on the horizon, his thoughts returned to that morning's departure from his wife and young children gathered at the end of the pier. Outside, the rose firmament, which only minutes earlier had set fire to the shimmering waters, forsook his ship beneath a canopy of darkness. Inside, Cromwell lay on his bed, ready to encounter Morpheus as the captain of sleep.

As with all who in their youth are inclined to think that the scores of years that lie ahead are endless, Cromwell happily hummed to himself and prayed to the God of his Scots forbearers—the God who "creates, sustains, rules, and guides all things."

In quarters fit, not for the repose of a king, but for a yeoman attentive to noble ideals rather than to royal fetishes like shiny brass fixtures, vintage wines in crystal goblets, and china plates garnished with quail eggs and caviar, Cromwell drifted into the realm where dreams composed of fantasy soon awaken to the harsh realities of fact.

Suddenly, an abrupt knock at the door bolted the captain out of his slumber as a crew member shouted, "Captain! Captain! We're in trouble!"

"What is it?" the bleary-eyed skipper asked.

"It's a passenger liner. It's bearing down upon us, sir. Come quickly!"

By two leaps and a bound Cromwell scaled the ladder and peered out into the night.

Sure enough, deck lights reflecting from a shadowy, menacing hulk of steel could be seen approaching all too close to offer wide berth to the smaller wooden craft. There was little time to avoid an impending catastrophe. As the surging passenger liner drew clearer into view, its colossal bow induced panic.

"My God, it's going to hit us!" Cromwell shouted.

The captain ordered every woman, man, and child to take to the lifeboats. Within little more than the twinkling of an eye, all were huddled, shivering in the dinghies.

The seizure of chill took hold, less from the cold night air than from the paralysis of fear. Each lifeboat was packed to the gunnels with the flesh-and-bones drama of a living nightmare. A dread encounter-of-the-last-kind had struck with a vengeance. All watched in horror as their demolished ship sank beneath the surface.

Meanwhile, the lights of the passenger liner flickered into the distance until they faded into oblivion.

"Why? How could this have happened?"

"Who could be so cruel?"

"Where is sympathy for the little guy?"

"Why did that bully of a beast strike and then flee?"

"To whom do we now turn?"

"Where is the Almighty? Does God so little care? Are we to perish in this vast ocean of death?"

The captain was such a skillful raconteur that we, the eavesdroppers, upon hearing his recounting of the calamity, huddled on his living room floor as though we too were cowered with the crestfallen in the basins of the lifeboats.

Cromwell said that he was the only person among his crew and passengers who did not make it into one of them. He lay instead with his body parallel to the ocean's surface, with his arms outstretched above his head and his broad hands and gangly fingers grasping at the gunnel's edge.

"All at once," motioning with a sweep of his arm, he said, "I realized that I had lost everything—my ship, my house, my savings, my precious cargo, my dream. It all went to the bottom. And as I reached to feel the weight of my trousers pulling me down, I knew they had to go, too. I was naked before God.

"As the minutes and hours passed, there was no way to know whether we'd bake, or starve, or drown to death. Or whether by some fluke of fate perchance we would float off to some island paradise.

"So we prayed. We prayed desperately for our salvation."

The captain leaned forward in his chair, drawing closer to us as he pointed to something across the room, toward which we turned our heads.

"Now, you won't believe this," he said. "But over there in the distance, after half the night is spent, we see a flickering light appearing from the same direction in which the ocean liner had disappeared.

"Fact of the matter is, unless you'd been in those dark waters with us, you couldn't imagine how even the faintest ray of light way over yonder could give you the brightest glimmer of hope. We shouted for joy, even though we didn't know for sure that we could believe our eyes."

Yet it was true. The same shadowy, menacing hulk of steel, which had taken aim at the captain's wooden schooner and capsized it, returned to the scene of the crime, pulled alongside the lifeboats, raised their cheering occupants to safety, wrapped them in warm blankets, fed them, and delivered them to the port of Havana. To everyone's astonishment, however, the captain of the passenger ship refused to meet and greet the rescued refugees.

"But a very strange thing happened to me," said Cromwell.

"Several years later, after I had gotten myself back together and become the chief of a banana boat not of my possession, I docked at New Orleans where I ran into an acquaintance named Jones whom I had not seen for a while. He too was a captain in the merchant marine.

"Jones said that he had heard about my near disaster and wondered if I had ever received an explanation as to why the passenger liner turned back and rescued us. I said I had no idea, but it puzzled me greatly that any captain would hit and run.

"Then Jones asked me if I remembered a young woman standing on the bow of my freighter as the lifeboats were unleashed.

"'Indeed, I did,' I said. I can see her now, stationed in the shadows with her baby in arms. The child's cries still haunt me.

"So Jones gave me his version of what happened. I don't know where he got it, but he said, 'Well, Cromwell, you know it really was a very strange thing, but another woman was standing on the bow of the passenger liner. She, too, held a baby in her arms. When she saw what was about to happen to the young mother on the bow of your freighter, clinging to her child for dear life, she pictured herself and her own little one being in the same predicament.

"'So she ran immediately to speak with her captain and begged him to turn around and save your people. But her captain resolutely refused. And that made her so angry that she persisted in pestering him for several hours until at last she threatened him, saying, "If you don't turn around now, then when we get to Havana, I personally will see to it that you never sail your ship again!" And with that her captain got the message.'"

Shortly after having told those of us seated in his living room about his first day at sea as a captain, the beloved Thomas Cromwell suffered a heart attack and sailed his "earthen vessel" into the eternal deep.

This story was told at his funeral service to which crews of various races and tongues from ports where he had docked, and ships he had captained, came to honor him.

Captain Cromwell loved to tell this story because it answered mystery with mystery and left his listeners wondering just who his acquaintance in New Orleans, named Jones, really was.

Was Jones possibly the captain of the obscure, menacing passenger liner that had capsized Cromwell's schooner that fateful night at sea?

Which leads to another question . . .

Is God the irascible old he-captain of what Kipling called "that packet of assorted miseries which we call a Ship,"[4] who judges the Earth's inhabitants with unexplained

---

[4] Rudyard Kipling, *A Book of Words*, XV, "The First Sailor."

tempests of capricious and demonic fury, as though Satan himself could not have fallen as one of the angels if God had not permitted it?

Or, is this same God a she-captain who is quite determined that justice shall be done where justice is due, and that grace full of compassion will be vindicated on the face of the Deep as never before—the final victory of her continual coming and pleading and threatening and demanding that "love never ends"?

5

"Best and Deepest" Self-Portraits

"The soul is a mirror before it becomes a home."
From Alphonse de Lamartine's *Cromwell*
Quoted by Vincent van Gogh (1853–1890)
Letter 100 ~ June 5, 1877 ~ Amsterdam

IF ONE TAKES THE TIME to study Vincent van Gogh's numerous self-portraits, it is apparent that there are several "Vincents" dwelling within the one Vincent. Never, though, do Vincent's self-portraits exhibit an outright display of mirth. Like a hound tracking a faint whiff of exotic expectation, one must hunt for the glee hidden beneath the surface of Vincent's solemn countenance.

Yet, if his mirth is imperceptible within his mirrored visages, there is apparent nevertheless within the vast repertoire of his art and letters an ample supply of *unpainted* "self-portraits" intimating what Vincent often said of himself when reiterating the words of Saint Paul: "Sorrowful, yet always rejoicing."

As for the human subjects who sat before his discerning eye, Vincent declared: "I always feel confident when I am doing portraits, knowing that this work has much more depth—it isn't the right word perhaps, but it is what makes me cultivate whatever is best and deepest in me."[5]

---

[5] Johanna van Gogh-Bonger, editor, *The Complete Letters of Vincent van Gogh* 517, 2:625.

It seems the "best and deepest" that Vincent cultivated in himself, for having seen and depicted the "best and deepest" in others, became the wellspring from which he "drew" the crowning artistic achievements of his life. The entire array of his drawings and paintings, in a manner of speaking, contains implicit self-portraits. The depth of his innermost being permeated the depth he encountered beyond himself in the fullness of nature including human nature, whether in the thunderstruck sky or the sunlit face. Vincent as artist was integrally and resonantly connected to his subject. To stand before his art is to stand before the soul of both.

From the nearly 900 Van Gogh still life, landscape, seascape, and "peoplescape" paintings that may be alternately viewed as projective renditions of aspects of Vincent's inner subjectivities, for those viewers who keep their eyes peeled there also emerge before them more than a few veiled images of the holy and mysterious One—the Artist—whose enshrouded appearances are principally and sublimely joyful. This may explain in part the consolation so widely derived from the mindful observation of Vincent's art.

Vincent's succinctly stated sacral mission was this: "In a picture I want to say something comforting, as music is comforting. I want to paint men and women with that something of the eternal which the halo used to symbolize, and which we seek to convey by the actual radiance and vibration of our coloring."[6]

Just so, and truer than all the lesser parts of him that contradict or conceal his deepest self, Vincent's truest self continues even today to break forth upon many a captivating canvas like a burst of sunlight at dawn. Or, to re-image the epiphany, his brush and pigment unleash his

---

[6] *The Complete Letters* 531, 3:25.

quintessential self like a pageant of bright shining stars dazzling the midnight sky.

Whether we ponder the convergence of darkness and light swirling through the fireworks of his "Starry Night," or fine-tune our attention to the soulful essence of his portraits of an Agostina Segatori or a Joseph Roulin, it is as we linger in their presence by means of prolonged meditation that we encounter sacred dimensions of life inherent in everyday people.

As for Vincent's idiosyncratic self-portraits, set alongside his portrayals of those iconic persons who sat for their portraits in front of his sympathetic easel, there is always more depth to be found in their countenances than what meets the first glance of a viewer's eye.

Remarkably, to undertake an in-depth study of the celebrated Dutchman's art and letters is also to embark upon a comparable study, as it were, of ourselves. For, just as Vincent said that painting portraits was "what makes me cultivate whatever is best and deepest in me," so does our immersion in his artistic and literary imagination cultivate whatever is "best and deepest" in us.

6

"Follow Me When I Try to Explain Something"

"Being heard is so close to being loved that for the average person, they are almost indistinguishable."

—David W. Augsburger, *Caring Enough to Hear and Be Heard*[7]

VINCENT VAN GOGH once wrote of his father with whom he had more than one verbal altercation while living under the same roof, "I seem to detect in Father proofs . . . of his really being unable to follow me when I try to explain something to him. He clings to a part of what I say, which becomes incorrect when one tears it from its context. This may have more than one cause, but assuredly it is largely the fault of old age."[8]

Old age aside, rather than decrying his father's inability to follow what Vincent attempted to explain to him, suppose Vincent instead had inquired of his father: "What is it like for you when I'm conversing with you, and you with me?"

Had Vincent posed such a question without accusation or rejoinder, his father might have taken pause, even pleasure, in reflecting with Vincent about his son's wish to be better understood. By entering his father's frame of

---

[7] David W. Augsburger, *Caring Enough to Hear and Be Heard* (Ventura: Regal Books, 1982), 12.
[8] *The Complete Letters* 347, 2:239.

reference, Vincent may have learned something important about his father as well as about himself.

Vincent's retorts were often if not always rigid, forceful, and argumentative, thus hard to bear, especially when his precipitous outbursts of rage interrupted the flow of communication, as happened in relation to his father, his brother Theo, and others who kept his company.

The devilish truth was that neither father nor son knew how best to attune emotionally to the other's presence and thereby offer sufficient mutual affirmation and validation to avoid struggling so intensely with each other's spirit. It was less demanding yet far less productive for them to remain outwardly defensive by shadowboxing rather than moving inwardly with empathy and sensitivity toward each other's experienced reality. But, then, how to begin?

Seeking meaningful engagement with a wounded soul who is in pain and suffering warrants close observation of the sufferer's face, eyes, and voice. For in the visage one can "follow" the contours of distress or, conversely, the expressions of relief that emerge from within.

Affect is key. By analogy, affect is to speech as music is to the lyrics of song, either concordant or discordant with the content of the words. In human relationships "empathic attunement"[9] is essential for discerning in the moment of encounter the other person's state of mind, heart, and soul.

When a ray of light suddenly breaks forth from a person's prison of gloom, darkness, or distress, thanks to feeling profoundly understood, that ray appears in the face, the eyes, and the tone of voice. What often occasions it is

---

[9] "Empathic attunement" is a psychoanalytic concept and therapeutic method defined and developed by the psychoanalyst Heinz Kohut, M.D., who wrote: "The best definition of empathy . . . is that it is the capacity to think and feel oneself into the inner life of another person." Heinz Kohut, *How Does Analysis Cure* (Chicago: University of Chicago Press, 1984), 82.

the very thing that Vincent craved most of all for himself and yet found inordinately difficult to grant to his father, as when Vincent in his own words said, "follow me when I try to explain something," which is to say, offer me your powers of undivided attention, of careful observation and deep listening.

The face, the eyes, and the tone of voice comprise the canvas upon which the soul paints its pictures of what is essential for personal acknowledgment and the resultant feeling of being genuinely understood.

Especially is this evident, as it was between Vincent and his father, when things heated up to the point where Vincent summarily declared to his father, "Pa, here I am faced by your self-righteousness, which was and is fatal, for you as well as for me." Whereupon his father instantly retorted, "Do you expect me to kneel before you?"[10]

That was clearly a point at which the mutual train of empathy—"follow me when I try to explain something"—fell off track.

Grace took a nasty tumble into the cocklebur.

—Which serves to underscore the fact that one of the profoundest gifts of grace a person can give another is to attend with undivided attention, careful observation, and deep listening for the sake of reaching the moment of real understanding.

It is a gift that all who are in the healing professions need to cultivate.

---

[10] *The Complete Letters* 345a, 2:231.

7

"From Warriors to Saints, Saints to Lovers, Lovers to Tigers, Tigers to Flowers"

They came to Jericho. . . Bartimaeus son of Timaeus, a blind beggar was sitting by the roadside. . . Then Jesus said to him, "What do you want me to do for you?" The blind man said to him, 'My teacher, let me see again.' Jesus said to him, "Go; your faith has made you well." Immediately he regained his sight. —Mark 10:46–52

VINCENT VAN GOGH LEARNED VOLUMES from his fellow artists by the study of countless numbers of their drawings and paintings, some old, some new. Not only did he visit many museums and exhibitions. He also lined the walls of his room with copies of others' works, including the great masters who preceded him.

Vincent once wrote to his brother Theo:

I must ask you something: Are there any cheap Daumier prints to be had, and, if so, which ones? I always found him very clever, but it is only recently that I have begun to have the impression that he is more important than I thought. If you know any particulars about him or if you have seen any of his important drawings, please tell me about it . . . I remember we spoke about it last year on the road to Prinsenhage, and you said then that you like Daumier better than Gavarni, and I took Gavarni's part, and told you about the book I had read about Gavarni which you have now. But I must say that since then, though I have not come to like Gavarni less, I begin to suspect that I know but a very small portion of Daumier's work and that the very things which would interest me most are *in the portion of his work which I do not know.*[11]

Are there any parallels to us?

All learning takes place at the intersection of what we already know and what we do not yet know. An artist can interpret *only what the artist presently sees*. The same is true for the therapist conducting therapy, the surgeon performing surgery, or the politician crafting legislation. To that end, personal and professional consultation offers fresh eyes with which to see and novel ears with which to hear.

A patient and a therapist, the two of them, working collaboratively may generate what is called an "analytic third"[12]—an additional and potentially constructive or transformative perspective emerging from the juxtaposition of their two separate realities. That is, the patient has "one" subjective experience (say, a fantasy) and the therapist a "second" subjective experience (say, a daydream) in relation to the patient's experience, which when coming together form an intersubjective "pair" or "third" experience, which opens the way to new and deeper meanings and understandings.

Apply this to the artist generating art by encountering other artists and their art. What if Vincent had remained only in his own head and his own experience as developed

---

[11] *The Complete Letters* 239, 1:474.
[12] A phenomenological concept developed by psychoanalyst Thomas H. Ogden, M.D., "The Analytic Third: Working with Intersubjective Clinical Facts," *The International Journal of Psychoanalysis* 75 (February 1994) 1:3-19.

at home among the many Dutch artists with whom he was acquainted? Imagine what growth might *not* have occurred for him as an artist if, in addition to those endeavors, he had not studied Japanese art and French Impressionist paintings.

What if he had never made his way to Paris and subsequently to the south of France where the sun shone brighter than it did back in the Netherlands?

One of the most dramatic transformations of Vincent's artistic style and subject matter came about with his turn to the use of vivid colors as a consequence of his modified geographic perspective.

Likewise, when he studied the art of those with whom he was unfamiliar, he further opened himself to the possibility for substantive changes of perspective and technique. It is just so with those of us who become absorbed in Vincent's art. We stand to encounter an "*artistic* third" bearing for us an altered perception. We begin to see things in our own mind that were not possible to see before, and not only of Vincent's reality as he painted it, but of what suddenly appears in our imaginations, thoughts, and dreams as a result of, say, standing wide-eyed before his glorious "Starry Night."

An old man once remarked to me that he had a wall-size reproduction of it hanging in his living room. Why so? Because, he said, "every day I sit before it and contemplate what it is like to be in heaven."

That was his "artistic third."

* * *

Consider again what Vincent said about the French painter Honoré Daumier while Vincent was still living and painting in the Netherlands in 1882: "If you [Theo] know any particulars about him or if you have seen any of his important drawings, please tell me about it . . . I know but a very small portion of Daumier's work and that the very things which would interest me most are *in the portion of his work which I do not know.*"

Whether we are therapists or surgeons or politicians, or anything else by virtue of art or craft or trade—whether we are the ones seeking "counsel" or the ones rendering it— what if we were to receive each new encounter as a creative and promising juxtaposition of what we already know with what we do not yet know?

What might happen?

Vincent mentioned Daumier in sixty-two of his letters. Three years after having asked Theo to tell him more about Daumier, Vincent wrote his friend Emile Bernard to say of yet another artist, in the words of the French writer, Théophile Silvestre, " 'Thus died—almost smiling— Eugène Delacroix, a painter of high breeding—who had a sun in his head and a thunderstorm in his heart—who went from warriors to saints—from saints to lovers—from lovers to tigers—and from tigers to flowers.'" Then Vincent added, "Daumier is also a great genius."[13]

What if Vincent had failed to ask Theo to tell him more about Daumier? On the other hand, what if we, like Vincent, were to ask those around us to help us gain a new perspective upon our present reality so that we might move beyond it to something potentially more significant?

What if we were to obtain that "analytic" or "*artistic third*" offering us the ability to paint life differently?

What if the person with whom we are currently engaged in conversation says to us, "Here is what I see. So, have you considered *this*? Have you considered *that*?"

---

[13] *The Complete Letters* B13, 3:506.

What if, thereby, we are no longer limited to "the world according to Gavarni" or the world according to "*Gutenough*," as good as those worlds may be?

What if we were to see the world and paint it as did, say, Jesus of Nazareth? or the Buddha? or Mahatma Gandhi? or Mohammed? or Julian of Norwich? or Mother Teresa? or Martin Luther King Jr.? or Rosa Parks? or Vincent van Gogh?

One can confidently conclude in the case of Van Gogh that his psychotic "break*down*," which took place within the presence of Paul Gauguin just before Christmas 1888, bore elements of an "artistic third." Such an experience, painful and debilitating though it was, eventually precipitated a "break*through*" of such stellar proportion that in the final year of his life, with *searing new eyes*, he was able to depict on canvas his vision of the new heaven and new earth that he had contemplated as a young man during frequent and studious encounters with the Jesus of the Gospels.

Yes, that's right. Jesus offers a new vision for the old life.

Whom, then, did Vincent have reason to thank for his epiphanies? Theo? Gavarni? Daumier? Delacroix? Gauguin? The coal miners in the coal mines of the Borinage? All of the above? Any others?

But what if he had never so much as once encountered Jesus—or worse—in doing so, he had failed to take the Nazarene seriously?

So—what if, from the perspective of the persons seated next to *us*, with whom we have momentarily cast our lot, we unexpectedly discover brand new takes on reality? Might we then no longer be exactly the same persons today that we were yesterday?

Can you imagine an artist painting canvas after canvas without ever shifting visual perspective? What kind of art would such constraint produce? Yet, when we look around,

51

and all too often when we look within, we realize just how stuck we are in the same old hardened perspectives and patterns, time and again. It's true of therapists, patients, surgeons, and politicians.

On the contrary—can you imagine shifting "from warrior to saint, from saint to lover, from lover to tiger, from tiger to flower," with each transmutation bearing the novel perspective of "a sun in the head, and a thunderstorm in the heart"?

And to what end? That our darkened and crazed souls might be awakened to a radically new way of perceiving, being, and acting in the world.

Yes, even to the extent that at the hour of our death, with the curtain pulled back from the face of death itself, and with our mortal remains reposing in astonishment like those of Delacroix, we might jolly well appear "almost smiling," mightn't we?

Therefore, when imprisoned within those calcified perspectives that impede warriors from becoming saints, saints lovers, lovers tigers, and tigers flowers, then for heaven's sake why would we not welcome unfamiliar vistas that we have not yet encountered?

Jesus said, "Ask, and it will be given you; search, and you will find; knock, and the door will be opened to you" (Matt 7:7).

That was his bold invitation to receive the "artistic third."

Once in a while, with a sun in the head and a thunderstorm in the heart, warriors become saints who love like tigers clutching a bouquet of flowers.

By the searing new eyes of grace.

8

"A World of Surprises"

"There lives the dearest freshness deep down things;
And though the last lights off the black West went
Oh, morning, at the brown brink eastward, springs—
Because the Holy Ghost over the bent
World broods with warm breast and with ah! Bright wings."
—Gerard Manley Hopkins (1844–1899), "God's Grandeur"

BEING MOTHER OR FATHER to your own life's work is like the stone-deaf Beethoven birthing the Ninth Symphony's *Ode to Joy*. The craft of creativity is far more formidable than comprehensible. We become infinitely more dependent upon what we do not know than upon what we know.

Who knows for sure whether this score will ever make sense or sound?—as Beethoven surely must have plagued himself in fruitful self-doubt while laboring over a multitude of musical phrases.

We, deeply stirred by the sound and sense of Beethoven's muse, must ask a question. Are we the sole proprietors of our works? Unlike clocks ticking in a hushed universe, are we swept along by something far more compelling than the ill-fated motions of hands and faces gradually winding down? How do we, being at times so mortally hard of hearing, like Beethoven, become at other times acutely attuned, oddly enough, to the sounds of silence that strangely disrupt our imperviousness to grace?

What comedy amid tragedy! Here is Beethoven arranging the musical harmony of one of the most sublime moments of his life—an entire symphony. Yet he's composing the riches of a majestic melody to the dread, awful contradiction of absolute, mute silence.

Henry van Dyke sought words for the *Ode*: "Joyful, joyful, we adore Thee, God of glory, Lord of love." And Beethoven, it is ascribed, also composed seven measures of a chant for an offertory response. "All things come of Thee, O Lord, and of thine own have we given Thee."

Enter upon the scene.

You, music lover, take a deliberate glance at the deeply entranced Beethoven. By fits and starts he is sitting with his muse. His "time" has caught up with him. The years immediately preceding have been overwhelmed with anxiety and grief, his output brief. But now comes one of those "given" instants, most would say, of brilliance. The master musician is composing his *Joy* in eerily deafened silence, yet the moon and the tides are waxing eloquently.

Is unbridled faith able to muffle the world's screaming dissonance long enough for anyone to listen and know that it is none other than *God* who speaks?

Ludwig, alone yet not alone, "hears" the music of the spheres as the presence of *None Other*. Are we surprised?

Mundane explanations aside, is it not forever true that "of thine own have we given Thee"? Did Beethoven love God all the more for not being able to hear the chanting cardinals and warbling snowbirds awaken him in the morning? Did their sound waves inaudibly split the air of his silent universe, mysteriously entering the marrow of his bones that he might declare in song, "O God!"?

The rest of us, as uninspired mimics of the world's misfortunes, may be less than attentive if we possess all our faculties, save one. We in the digital age, perhaps permanently, have lost the quiet composure for staying still long enough, first to dream and imagine and then to sing Beethoven's joyous melody *close in* for one solitary split second. The world of immediate bellow and clamor has dulled our inner senses. Our spirits have sprung loose like frayed violin strings. If only our flagging souls were to commit the art of our living to the deaf side of our being, we might be surprised at what we hear when silenced like stone.

One day, early on, before his ears were hardened to the vibrations of perceptible melody, the young Ludwig was handed the task of learning to play the piano. What if there had been no piano? Would an "enthused" Ludwig have had the presence of heart, like an oyster, to take up pearl making? Mark Twain once quipped, "It is a world of surprises. They fall, too, where one is least expecting them."[14]

* * *

Consider the child Mozart. Full of gift, full of surprise, his "lyrics" were pure "liquid sunshine,"[15] or, as Karl Barth honored him by saying, "he heard the harmony of creation to which the shadow also belongs but in which the shadow is not darkness, deficiency is not defeat, sadness cannot become despair. trouble cannot degenerate into tragedy, and infinite melancholy is not ultimately forced to claim undisputed sway. Thus the cheerfulness in this harmony is

---

[14] Mark Twain, "Chapters Begun in Vienna," *The Autobiography of Mark Twain*, Vol. 1 (Project Gutenberg), 144. https://standardebooks.org.
[15] In his April 1, 1974 conversation with the author, George A. Buttrick ascribed the term "liquid sunshine" to Karl Barth as Barth's way of describing Mozart's music.

not without its limits. But the light shines all the more brightly because it breaks forth from the shadow."[16]

Yet Mozart's life remained tumultuous. What, then, explained his music? In the midst of Wolfgang's gathering storm, how on Earth was he able to compose such implausible reverberations of grace? Was it by lunacy that he achieved ethereal heights? To what end? Only so that he could be cast into an unmarked pauper's grave, his lot thrown in with the rest of us?

Oh, "liquid sunshine," like that yellow ball of fire in the sky, how quickly you fade to the west, wearing out your heart in the fever of darkness!

Mozart exhausted his song. His song exhausted Mozart. In his thirty-fifth year the virtuoso perished, not having completed his life's last measure of mirth. Had he lived yet a few more, then what? Maybe not nearly so much. For what is life when measured by years? Among the last words that Amadeus, "lover of God," penned to his unfinished Requiem were these: "Make them pass from death to life."

Truth is, each day is a divine-human "passage." In "a world of surprises" belonging first to God before being found of us in ways we least expect, each day is a passage "from death to life."

Come, close your eyes and see. Come, close your ears and hear. Like chanting cardinal and warbling snowbird, come open your heart and sing with whatever song you are given grace to say thanks.

---

[16] Karl Barth, Geoffrey William Bromiley, and Thomas Forsyth Torrance, *Church Dogmatics, III, 3* (Edinburgh: T. and T. Clark, 1936), 298n.

9

The Incomparable Tooney

"The lady doth protest too much, methinks."
—Hamlet to Queen Gertrude of Denmark, Shakespeare
(1564–1616), "Hamlet" III, ii

———————

SHE WAS A TIRED, worn-out old woman to whom nobody would listen. Morning, noon, and night, moment after moment, her sole song consisted of the same old forlorn refrain as she moaned the same old woebegone verse, *"Nurse! Nurse! Come down here, Nurse! Where is you anyway? Come down here. Nurse!"*

It was my first day as a clinical pastoral intern on the general medical ward of Grady Memorial Hospital in Atlanta. My pastoral charge was to visit each patient in every room, up one side of the corridor and down the other, gently knocking at each door, saying, "Good morning, Mr. Blue. Good afternoon, Mrs. Bright. I'm Charles Davidson. I'm the chaplain on this floor. May I take a moment to introduce myself and visit with you?"

Without saying so, some thought to themselves, "Oh, my God, the chaplain! Am I dying?"

Others spoke with approval, "I'm glad to see you. Thank you for coming."

A few responded with polite rebuttal, "No, thank you. I don't believe so."

Gradually, throughout the morning's and afternoon's initiation, I made my rounds from room to room, five minutes here and fifteen minutes there, then again for half an hour or so when the family had gathered or when the tide of events had turned toward the shoreline and there was no more beachfront left for making sand castles or for allowing one's thoughts to drift to sea since the clouds had fallen low.

Then, too, during the days and weeks that followed, there was that random interruption when the pager summoned me to the consultation room or to the ER, such as when a bone surgeon called me to ask if I would be willing to meet with one of his patients to convince her that she needed to have her leg amputated lest gangrene kill her off should she refuse to give consent to surgery.

I said, of course, I would be glad to visit her but that my job was not to convince. It was to listen, reflect, pose appropriate questions, and pray when prayer was in the asking.

As it turned out, toward the end of my conversation with her, she confided a secret that I was not to share with the doctor or anyone else until after surgery. Without question, she wanted to live, and she had few qualms about undergoing the knife. But before she would give her consent, she said she had to go home to tend to some business that was hers and hers alone to finish, and would I please tell the doctor that that's the way it was going to be, which I did.

She was released to go home for two days, where she met her only son who flew in from another city. There she showed him exactly where her life's savings were buried in the back yard, and then she returned to the hospital for the amputation.

Days later, she thanked me for having prayed with her before the bloody ordeal, as she lay on her bed trying to figure out how she was going to make it for the rest of her life with only one leg left to stand on. So she asked me to pray again.

Being the musically-inclined pastor that I was, if only I had had the presence of mind to sing so, I would have suggested that we join together in that old African American spiritual, "It's me, it's me, O Lord, standing in the need of prayer," since surely, she knew it by heart.

A former slave once said, "I pray now and just tell God to take me and do his will, for he knows every secret of my heart. He knows what we stand most in need of before we ask for it, and if we trust him, he will give us what we ought to have in due season."[17]

* * *

All the while that I moved about the general medical ward, introducing myself as the new chaplain on the "block," I heard that tired, worn-out old songster wailing for all she was worth, as far from the nurses' station as they could keep her out of sight if not out of mind.

"Nurse! Nurse! Come down here, Nurse! Where is you anyway? Come down here, Nurse!"

Finally, I had had all I could take of not knowing what lay behind this incomparable woman's summons for help. Perhaps it was her way of praying without ceasing. If so, then I should not judge her otherwise. So I marched up to the nurses' station and asked what was going on with the woman at the end of the hall.

"Oh, that's Tooney!" the nurse said. "She's just that way. No matter how many times we go in to see her, she keeps calling for us."

---

[17] Clifton H. Johnson, *God Struck Me Dead: Voices of Ex-Slaves* (Eugene, OR: Wipf & Stock, 1969, 2013), 58.

"Well, do you mind if I take a turn?"

"No, go right ahead. Maybe you can get somewhere with her."

So, with trepid heart, I stepped into choppy waters without wearing a life jacket, and headed toward Tooney's room.

Parenthetically, while Tooney has long since found her treasure in heaven some forty or more years ago, I withhold her surname out of respect for the privacy of her family, and for fear that if I were to reveal it now, Tooney just might decide to come back to haunt me in my old age since in her mind, in some manner of speaking, my un-preacherly presence must have haunted her.

So there I was, the chaplain, standing in the need of prayer myself, tapping on Tooney's door which stood wide open. And there she sat, placidly for such a doggedly determined old soul, strapped into her hospital armchair by a white sheet tied around her waist.

She looked up at me as if stunned with sudden disbelief, incredulous that someone, anyone, had actually answered her cry and "come down here" to see her.

I paused before I took another step. For in full view of my disbelieving eyes, Tooney exhibited the most God-awful gash across her forehead, deep into her flesh, with blood oozing down upon her frail brown brow (I later discovered why) due to her being singed to the skull bone by having fallen face-first into a blazing fire in the fireplace of her deep South Georgia home.

As I winced, and before I could so much as say my name to introduce myself, she flipped me a question.

"You got any Life Savers?"

"No, Ma'am, I'm sorry, I don't."

"Well, why don't you have any Life Savers? And who *is* you? I ain't never seen you befo'.""

"I'm Charles Davidson, the chaplain, Ma'am."

"The *who?*"

Clearly, she didn't comprehend. So I translated with my own broken southern lingo as best I could into words I figured she'd understand for sure.

"I'm the *preacha*, Ma'am."

But saying that was like striking coal in a gold mine.

"*Suh, you ain't no preacha. You might think you is. But if you keeps wurkin' at it, some days you might jes be's one!*"

For the next several weeks and for the entire time she was hospitalized—tied to her chair and still beckoning at the top of her lungs for the nurses to "come down here"— whenever I set foot into her room, the very first words out of her mouth were "You got any Life Savers?"

No matter what we talked about, or for how long, or how often we repeated the same conversation, in as much as I had to re-introduce myself each time as the chaplain, she never believed me to be the chaplain or the *preacha*.

From the first day until the last, in her mind she was busy rocking herself in her old wooden rocking chair on the front porch of her home in South Georgia, and insisting— who would have guessed it?—that I was the *milkman*.

When I reported my fortuitous initial encounter with Tooney to our clinical training peer group, I did so in the form of a written verbatim that set forth what had transpired between us as I walked into her room that propitious day, and she said, "*Suh, you ain't no preacha. You might think you is. But if you keeps wurkin' at it, some days you might jes be's one!*"

My supervisor turned to me and with a twinkle in his eye posed a question.

"Do you think she was trying to tell you something?"

10

John's Garden

Is it not to share your bread with the hungry, and bring the homeless poor into your house . . . Then your light shall break forth like the dawn and your healing shall spring up quickly . . . Then you shall call, and the Lord will answer; you shall cry for help, and he will say, Here I am.

—Isaiah 58:7–9

SOUTHMINSTER PRESBYTERIAN was a small suburban congregation in Daytona, Florida, about as ordinary as any church on any corner in any city, so much so that you might not even have noticed it when driving by.

Its pastor, Dan Taylor, was my seminary classmate and for thirty-nine years like a brother to me until his untimely death of cancer at age sixty. Long after he had moved on to become a pastoral counselor, he was reminiscing about his years at Southminster. Among his most vivid memories, one stood above them all. It pertained to a man named John, who had wandered off the street one day and into the church.

There was no secret to the fact that John was an alcoholic. He made no secret of it himself. John was a hobo, a vagabond, who rode the rails all over the country, hopping from one freight train to another.

The only personal belongings he had to his name were the clothes on his back and the bicycle he rode when he wasn't either walking afoot or leaning against the inside wall of a box car.

John had stopped at Southminster Church because he was hungry and needed food. He said that he was willing to work for pay if the church would give him something to do. So, being the ever-compassionate person that he was, my friend Dan gave John the job of tidying up the church grounds.

Off and on over the course of weeks that turned into months and several years, John went about tending the church's flowerbed, pulling the weeds, watering and manicuring the shrubs, and doing whatever needed to be done. Then he would take off on one of his railway excursions for an extended period of time while leaving his bicycle in storage at the church. Dan faithfully paid him for his work until John returned to perform his chores again.

Because John possessed sores and scabs all over his arms, due to years of imbibing alcohol, his physical appearance was somewhat off-putting. Simply speaking, it was painful to look at him.

Most of the church members who had met John were a bit afraid of him and didn't mind saying so. A few complained that John had no business being there, and that he certainly should not be allowed to work in the garden. After all, it was the church's garden and not John's garden.

Dan explained to them that if they were to take the time to get to know John, they would discover him to be "a very caring soul."

* * *

One day, Dan commented to John that the church really needed some small rocks to place around the garden.

"Oh, Dan," exclaimed John, "I know exactly where I can get you some rocks!" Sure enough, a few days later here comes John carrying a sack of rocks on his bicycle.

John was accustomed to spending most of his Daytona nights under a gazebo on the public golf course, down the middle of which ran a railroad track. So, without his saying so, it was not hard to imagine where the rocks came from.

During their many conversations, John never got around to telling Dan his last name. Perhaps John didn't want anyone to know who he was or where he was from. Maybe John's past was simply too much to reveal for fear that no one would understand or have the least bit of compassion for him.

But on one particular occasion, John began to tell Dan about his father who had lived up in the mountains of North Georgia, which turned out to be the icebreaker that opened the way to share some of the scarred and painful memories that John would just as soon have forgotten if he could. And then John set off roving the country on yet another freight train.

* * *

From time-to-time, Dan received a long-distance phone call from John, usually because John had been thrown into jail for loitering in a state of drunkenness or for having gotten into a brawl with someone.

John frequently spent a week or two behind bars, which gave him ample opportunities to write letters to Dan. And in those letters John inserted various drawings that he had made for Dan.

Dan said that he wished so much that he had kept those letters and drawings. But, as is so often the case, we fail to see the lasting value of something even when it stares us straight in the face.

65

As the luck of the draw would have it, after not hearing from John for a while, Dan received a phone call from a police detective in West Palm Beach.

"Is this Southminster Presbyterian Church?"

"Yes, it is."

"Are you Reverend Taylor?"

"Yes, I am."

"We are calling about a man we are unable to identify."

The detective described the man and asked, "Do you know him, Reverend Taylor?"

"Yes, I know him."

"Do you know his name?"

"Yes, his name is John. But I don't know his last name."

Dan told the detective how John had been working on and off around the church for two years, during which John frequently took off to ride the rails.

"Reverend Taylor, John was hit by a train here in West Palm. He died in the freight yard. In his pocket we found a bulletin from your church. That's how we knew to call you. We will bury him in a pauper's grave here in West Palm."

Dan hung up the phone. The silence was deafening.

* * *

The following Sunday morning, at eleven o'clock, the congregation of Southminster Presbyterian Church held a memorial service for John, during which Dan said there was not a single dry eye to be seen anywhere in the congregation.

Southminster had been John's only home, his sanctuary, his saving refuge. It was the one place he knew to call when the chips were down and his luck had run out.

After telling me this story as we sat together, Dan posed a question and we fumbled for an answer.

What do you suppose was at the center of John's life?

Was it the alcohol? The freight trains he hopped? The bicycle he stored at the church? The journeys he took for their own sake as he traveled the rails? The odd jobs he found along the way to buy food and clothing? The scarred and painful memories he carried of the past? The jailhouses in which he spent lonesome days and nights? The church bulletin he carried in his pocket? His conversations with Dan? Southminster Church itself? Or its garden brimming with bright flowers and manicured shrubs surrounded by those rail-bed rocks to which John returned to tidy up after his expeditions to the far country?

* * *

Soon after the Sunday morning memorial service for John, the elders and congregation of Southminster Church gathered on a solemn occasion beneath the Florida sun and held a ceremony of remembrance in the garden that the church officially named "John's Garden."

The prophet Isaiah spoke a word for just such a time.

"If you remove the yoke [of the burden] from among you, the pointing of the finger, the speaking of evil, if you offer your food to the hungry and satisfy the needs of the afflicted, then your light shall rise in the darkness and your gloom be like the noonday. The Lord will guide you continually, and satisfy your needs in parched places, and make your bones strong; and you shall be like a watered garden, like a spring of water, whose waters never fail" (Isa 58:9b–11).

Saint Paul, who was familiar with his own waters of travail after been baptized in the water of the Spirit, put it another way.

"We do not live to ourselves, and we do not die to ourselves. If we live, we live to the Lord, and if we die, we die to the Lord; so then whether we live or whether we die, we are the Lord's. For to this end Christ died and lived again, so that he might be Lord of both the dead and the living" (Rom 14:7–9).

It was true for John.

And it's true for you and me.

11

Portraits of You

For those persons with whom as their pastor or therapist I had the privilege of sitting and listening, and praying beneath my breath, "Oh, God!"

AS THE SAYING GOES, and as you have heard it said, you are the food you eat, the clothes you wear, the friends you make, the name you bear, the words you speak. You are also your social security number, your high school senior picture, the glimpse a passerby catches of you, and the epithet etched upon your tombstone.

Not least, you are what you see and think of yourself for better or worse when you look in the mirror and either sigh with satisfaction or scream in dismay. You are what you reconstruct of yourself at the end of your days when you add up the balance sheet and subtract the failures from the achievements and trust the sum total to be greater than zero. In that sense you are what you forget as well as what you remember.

You are also the person who has an honest conversation with yourself about not always being your best self, and needing more often than not to be your forgiving self. And when you are your false self, you are that part of yourself that hides from the rest of you your true self.

When you are your true self, you may hardly know exactly who you are, for in truth every true self is a composite of more than one self. You are several selves resident in one, and one centered at the heart of many.

Today you feel rotten, tomorrow on top of the world, which means you are somewhere within the vast range of normal. When the wind blows right and you go left, you are the person who discerns the difference between what is right for you and wrong for others. You respectfully leave it to them to know their own minds, even as you trust they will kindly leave it to you to make up yours.

You are a blundering idiot when you cannot help yourself, and a surprising wonder when you entrust yourself to the wisdom buried deep within you.

You are the sacred ground you tread upon, the holy sights you see, and the mystical things you do. You are the lover who, being loved, loves, and yet the one who can miss the mark of love altogether.

You are the hilarious moments you stumble upon that lift your spirit, and the horrendous deeds you witness that diminish your soul.

You are the prayers you say as you fall asleep, and the dreams you live before and after you awake.

Yes, all of these are portraits of you.

Yet even more, you are the living image of the One who made you the exquisite glory you are by God's extravagant grace.

PART TWO | Seasons

12

Quiet, Please! While the Fox Is Passing!

"Against the Word the unstilled world still whirled
About the centre of the silent Word."

—T. S. Eliot (1888–1965), "Ash Wednesday, V"

AMONG THE PURPORTED BLESSINGS of life in the countryside is nature's primordial gift of tranquility. This is reason enough to take the wilderness trail that rambles toward Eden.

To a human actor too long accustomed to the raucous rattle of the internal combustion engine in its endless procession over miles of concrete freeway, the world-stage of woods and stream with its hushed panorama of starlit nights and morning mists on the distant horizon is welcome respite for a pilgrim seeking solace for the soul.

This is not to say that nature is as well endowed with silence as it once was in that time-before-time when the Earth was a prehistoric habitat minus creation's crowning achievement, *homo sapiens* (the "wise guy"), whose penchant for disrupting the reigning serenity with all manner of congestion and noise is among an earthling's least admirable achievements. The presence of the human actor, on any stage, changes the disposition of the blue bird and the outlook of the fox, to say nothing of the godly lay of the land.

Believe it or not, but here in Campbell County, Virginia, those who have "generationed" among these rolling hills and farmlands are quite accustomed to the still-to-be-reckoned-with sound of the yelping foxhound driven by a drove of hungry hunters trotting around on horseback. Eager packs of dogs with their noses to the ground, numbering in the dozens, chase with passion through field and forest in unyielding pursuit of the forever sly but increasingly helpless old fox.

The sputter of the four-wheeled tractor and the screech of the earth-moving bulldozer have long since disturbed the fox's peace more than any natural, four-legged enemy ever did in the wild. Thus the fox by day, which once preyed upon the chicken as sport by night, can hardly find a lively henhouse anywhere that does not belong to the game of agribusiness, which in the free-market system has virtually eliminated the free reign of the chicken. In such diminished rural splendor, with beer can and wine bottle flung into nearly every roadside ditch, there is nevertheless, if but for a time, ample supply of the foxhound. It keeps the fox dizzily on the run from the hunter at its back while losing the battle against urban sprawl at its front.

* * *

My yellow Lab, Buddy, and I were on our early morning walk the other day in witness to the spring sunrise that was breaking over the horizon when we spotted the sleek gray form of a fox heading south down the tarmac road in front of us.

Its eyes turned back, glaring.

The fox was checking to see whether its symptomatic paranoia and depression were sufficient to warrant the fox doctor's diagnosis of a clinical disorder.

If I were the fox instead of the therapist, I would have prayed that the man and his dog keep the Prozac to themselves. Heaven forbid that pharmaceuticals find their way into the drinking water. For the last thing a fox needs is to be *drugged* into a state of euphoria as antidote to its lingering anxiety about the wiles of the human predator that repeatedly guns down the fox no matter where it attempts to hide.

Its's bad enough that the fox's collective unconscious is no longer able to remember a primordial age that was decidedly pre-anthropoidal. It will be even worse when the fox's best defense against extinction, its capacity to produce a birth rate higher than its death rate, no longer works in its favor. To be sure, utter disaster will prevail when the residual effect of "the morning after pill" in the drinking water puts an end to the fox's survival. No wonder the poor old fellow instinctively turns its head over its shoulder to see what's stalking it from behind. Yesterday it was the foxhound, today it's the polluted creeks and rivers.

Likewise, within the greater scheme of nature's changing state of tranquility, the rumble of the logging truck comes thudding and blundering around the bend in the road where I live, destined for chopping up and spitting out what's left of a pulp and paper economy in which the fast-growing pine supplants the slow-growing oak and maple.

The driver of the Big Mack, its friction decibels ascending in loud crescendo, careens his way down the road the fox has taken in quest of shrub and underbrush to conceal its bewilderment.

* * *

Subsequent to the primeval Fall, the road from Eden was first a fox alley, then the Natives' footpath, then a horse-and-buggy mud track, then a chuckhole-and-gravel road for the Model-T Ford, and then, come lately, a drag strip for the after-school racings of Generation Y in its red sports cars going nowhere faster than it goes everywhere by the Internet, thanks to the bighearted fossil fuel industry that supplies the gas and electricity.

Yes, I thank God for every vestige of quiet that prevails here within this oasis of "New Concord."

At the moment there is nothing stirring other than the gentle breeze fanning the pedals of the dogwood and the rustling leaf of the magnolia. Neither a cow moans in the distance nor a cloud billows over the mountain. There is deep silence in paradise for at least ten minutes.

Or, I should say, there *was* deep silence . . . for the carillon inside the white clapboard tower beneath the church steeple is abruptly blasting forth a song from the hymnal. Its bells are ripping through the stillness like the roar of a rocket headed for the hush of the moon. And dog Buddy, his snout to the sky, is howling for all he's worth in tune with the mighty Glory.

"Nearer, my God, to Thee, Nearer to Thee! Though like the wanderer, The sun gone down, Darkness be over me, My rest a stone: Yet in my dreams I'd be Nearer, my God, to Thee," wrote Sarah Adams in 1841, six years after this faithful congregation was founded.

"Nearer, my God, to Thee," did I say?

We pray Thee, yes. And, if so, then like the fox and the bluebird, who for the most part maintain their silence through all that is spinning around them, we draw our silence before God in the midst of the tumult by standing apart from it. For this is how God draws near to us, first apart and then close at hand.

Given that we have but fleeting acquaintance with the primordial gift of tranquility, wherever we are on this rambling wilderness trail in our return to Eden, when we pause long enough to listen—listen deeply—we detect below the surface noise a holy silence that is solace for the soul.

The secret is in the vigil of watching and listening—repeat—*watching and listening* to what flutters above it and shuffles below it at the very heart of nature—which is to say, to what is rousing from the depths of every living creature whom God knows by name and calls by name. Even the fox on the run that falls to the hunter, and the bluebird on the fly that fails to return to the nest, and the generations of the human species who fling their anxieties like empty beer cans and broken wine bottles into the far ditch as though there were no tomorrow over which to fret.

We know that we, too, will observe our silence in due time, when the Spirit is right, when at last the eye is able to see and the ear able to hear.

—O, Holy Silence.

13

The Bitter Frost and the Wild Snowflake

"Gather ye rose-buds while ye may,

Old Time is still a-flying;

And this same flower that smiles to-day,

To-morrow will be dying.

The glorious lamp of heaven, the sun,

The higher he's a-getting;

The sooner will his race be run,

And nearer he's to setting."

—Robert Herrick (1591–1674), "To the Virgins, to Make Much of Time"

———————

THE COLORFUL SPLENDOR that reigned supreme a month ago from mountain ridge to winding stream has morphed into something more ominous. Limbs and trunk are now but the cleft and gnarled skeletal remains of a cast of wooden characters that mime their misery with creepy arms and crooked legs stretched across low-slung clouds and the gray fog of autumn.

This year's bronze mat of decay lies sodden and fallow upon the forest floor. A gentle rain quenches the thirst of the famished earth.

We, the "pray-ers," having offered astonished thanksgiving for the elegant fall foliage, now find ourselves catching our breath in urgent petition for those among us whose wells have gone dry and brooks have dwindled to a trickle.

Grassy fields once alive with the verdant joys of summer have yielded up their vitality begrudgingly to pale russet dejection written upon the face of winter.

Stalwart evergreens brace themselves with solemnity against the fury of January winds that soon will cough up the bitter frost and the wild snowflake.

Across another continent, the "pray-ers" are war-torn and weary refugees of the current conflagration. They protrude empty stomachs while pleading for consolation from behind their veils of tears. The social and political landscape erupts in ruin and collapses in devastation with helpless children screaming and comfortless mothers sobbing in lament. The quaking of the ground sets fire to the face of the earth.

Into this whirling vortex, the Lord of creation makes entry and the spirit of Love is born. The good news, the promise of Isaiah, the hope of Advent, and the joy of Christmas is that he "has borne our griefs and carried our sorrows," and was "wounded for our transgressions" and "bruised for our iniquities" (Isa 53:4–5a).

No single person need lose hope.

In God's due season, the magnolia will blossom and the cherry tree send forth its fruit. For "the Lord has bared his holy arm before the eyes of all the nations; and all the ends of the earth shall see the salvation of our God" (52:10) to the relief of all suffering and the vanquishing of every injustice, including the sins of the good folk.

May such faith reign supreme through all the seasons of your heart.

14

Cry, Advent!

"Turning and turning in the widening gyre

The falcon cannot hear the falconer;

Things fall apart; the centre cannot hold;

Mere anarchy is loosed upon the world,

The blood-dimmed tide is loosed, and everywhere

The ceremony of innocence is drowned;

The best lack all conviction, while the worst

Are full of passionate intensity."

—Will Butler Yeats (1865–1939), "The Second Coming"

I DON'T RECALL JUST WHEN as a youngster I became aware of the purple season of Advent, until one day it leapt unannounced into my consciousness. Christmas, on the other hand, was marked by no such obscurity. In my toddling imagination, early in life I got the distinct impression that the season of glittering lights and the scent of Scots pine and Norway spruce would commence soon enough after we consumed the Thanksgiving turkey. 'Twas "the season to be jolly." Yet it ended all too shortly after Santa Claus came tumbling down the chimney.

Mingled among the enchantments were yummy baked sweets straight from the oven and brightly wrapped gift boxes neatly arrayed beneath the glossy ornaments and glistening tinsel that laced the Christmas tree.

Fused into the plot was the main cast of characters, the sanctified Mary and Joseph admiring the newly born Babe—all smiles, no cross yet in sight of the manger.

Luxuriating in the hay among the sheep and cows were the three regal wise men bearing forth their costly treasure, and a brightly shining star resplendent with heavenly wonder casting its sparkle Not least, a motley succession of Yuletide turtle doves, French horns, and "colly" birds.

Home from church on a Sunday afternoon in Advent, the radio blasted forth with the magical music of merry Noel—"I'm Dreaming of a White Christmas," "Here Comes Santa Claus," and the everlasting "Jingle Bells"—my favorite "hymns" at the time. Among them, "All I Want for Christmas Is My Two Front Teeth," in as much as by the age of five I had chipped off one-half of a front tooth while careening headlong into a garbage can.

But what I heard that morning in the sanctuary had largely passed me by, unnoticed, a contrarian chant, slow, measured, solemn, plaintive, its cadence steadily unwinding, upward then downward, its haunting lament like the plodding dirge of a band of mourners.

"O come, O come, Emmanuel, / And ransom captive Israel, / That mourns in lonely exile here / Until the Son of God appear. / O come Thou Dayspring, come and cheer / Our spirits by Thine advent here."

* * *

At the time, and in the place where I grew up, nothing else signaled Advent and Christmas quite so unmistakably as the ringing of the cash register. Mine, in the main, was a secure and uncomplicated childhood, apart from routine bumps and bruises.

It was not until the still tender age of nine that, with the swift chiming of the hour, I awakened from the dreamy sleep of my naïve innocence, peering dead-on into the "gloomy clouds of night."

I gawked into the jaws—since there's no other word to describe it—of *Hell.*

I was aghast . . . stunned . . . appalled.

God, please! or somebody, cover my eyes.

"White Christmas" abruptly turned dark and wistful. Santa Claus was stuck in the soot-lined chimney with one leg up and the other leg down in agony.

The red-nosed Rudolph, Prancer and Vixen, Comet and Cupid, Donner and Blitzen, had fallen headlong from their sleigh in the pillowed clouds of the sky.

Terror-stricken, I entered the season of Advent like a deer confronted by a leopard.

* * *

For the ancient sixth-century BC psalmist, the ordeal was epochal, perilous, and unmitigated, the result of what happens when an enemy pounces upon its prey.

"By the waters of Babylon, there we sat down and wept, when we remembered Zion. On the willow trees there we hung up our lyres. For there our captors required of us songs, and our tormentors, mirth, saying, 'Sing us one of the songs of Zion!'" But, "how shall we sing the Lord's song in a foreign land?" (Ps 137:1–4).

For twentieth-century Jews and others along with them who were dragged kicking and screaming from home and workplace, yet more often being forced into silent submission, the Diaspora of their forebear Jerusalemites foretokened the same dread doom all over again under the Nazi Reich.

To have been there in person would have been to bear witness in full-scale technicolor. What I saw with my eyes on the black and white television set was the stark cinematography the photographer had captured with the camera.

Many in my father's generation had come home from the war in shock and revulsion. They had seen firsthand for themselves the carnage of the concentration camps and gas chambers. For those in the liberating armies who had stumbled upon scenes of stacked skeletons of the dead and jam-packed cubicles of the scarcely living, the encounter with evil was more than breath-taking. It was repugnant, loathsome, and enraging.

One of my neighbors, a Jew, removed his shirt to show me the scars on his back from the ruthless torture he had endured during the unspeakable horrors of the Holocaust.

For me, a distant observer, the films of Dachau, Auschwitz, and Buchenwald were sufficient to sear a hole through my heart. I could not sleep for fear of the night itself.

I was nine years old, turning ninety-nine. Descending into that Netherworld, shuddering and cringing, I asked myself the same questions as nearly everyone else with a smidgeon of conscience.

How could this be?

How could anyone engage in such reprehensible, wholesale killing?

How could God allow for this?

How do God's children anywhere, whose bodies and spirits have bitten the dust—how do they possibly sing a carefree song of Advent, leading up to the "Halleluiah

Chorus" of Christmas, when the time at hand is one of grievous lament, when the spell of darkness prevailing over the season of light is like the leopard pouncing upon the deer?

What, then, do God's people do about this?

They cry. They cry, "Advent!"—

"O come, O come, Emmanuel, / And ransom captive Israel, / That mourns in lonely exile here / Until the Son of God appear. / O come Thou Dayspring, come and cheer / Our spirits by Thine advent here; / Disperse the gloomy clouds of night, / And death's dark shadows put to flight."

Paradoxically, Advent, as the season of exile and mourning, is precisely the time of God's coming—of "Emmanuel"—of "God with us."

The God of the manger *is* the God of the cross.

He, "who, though he was in the form of God, did not count equality with God a thing to be grasped, but emptied himself, taking the form of a slave, being born in human likeness . . . obedient unto death, even death on a cross" (Phil 2:6–8).

This is God's covenant. This is God's promise. This is the Crucified One in whom God has chosen to make common plight with us. And to all who have followed him into the most horrific situations the world can devise, his presence is the one thing, at times the only thing, that gives reason to sing, *"Rejoice! Rejoice!"*

For Emmanuel *has come* to thee, O Israel!

* * *

The late Jewish author, Elie Wiesel, recipient of the Nobel Peace Prize, as a teenager witnessed his own family perish in Auschwitz. Then, at Buna, he stood among the crowd and watched "three prisoners in chains," two men and a little boy, "the sad-eyed angel," led before the crowd to be hung in public view.

"All eyes were on the child. He was pale, almost calm, but he was biting his lips as he stood in the shadow of the gallows."

Someone standing behind Elie Wiesel asked the question, "Where is merciful God, where is He?"

"At the signal, the three chairs were tipped over. Total silence in the camp. On the horizon, the sun was setting."

The prisoners removed their caps. The boy, who said nothing, was the last to die after "for more than half an hour, lingering between life and death, writhing before our eyes."

Elie Wiesel concluded:

"Behind me I heard the same man asking: 'For God's sake, where is God?' And from within me, I heard a voice answer: 'Where he is? This is where—hanging here from this gallows.'"[18]

There are times in life and at death when we have no recourse except to trust the God who is with us, to trust God, the Crucified One, with all our life and with all our heart no matter where we are, no matter what has happened or what is about to happen—to trust God in our tears more than in our laughter—to trust God as we entrust the songs of our lyres to the weeping of the willow tree.

[18] Elie Wiesel, *Night* (New York: Hill and Wang, 1958, 2006), 64–65.

15

Christmas Trees

"O Christmas tree,
O Christmas tree,
How loyal are your needles.
You're green not only in the summertime,
No, also in winter when it snows.
O Christmas tree,
O Christmas tree
How loyal are your needles."
—Ernst Anschütz (1780–1861) "O Tannenbaum"

TO THIS DAY I still possess the handmade Santa Claus
that I cut out of lined poster board, colored with red crayon
for Santa's suit; black crayon for Santa's belt, boots, and left
glove; brown crayon for Santa's right glove; and pasted with
fluffy white cotton for Santa's sleeve cuffs, jacket hem, boot
tops, hat rim, and shaggy old head of hair and straggly beard.

My twelve-inch Santa Claus had graced the family Yule
tree every year since I had pinned his floppy limbs together
as a first-grader in 1950, until seven decades later when I
framed him inside a shadow box and hung him up for year-
round display on the wall next to the chimney.

One long-ago Christmas Eve, before I turned age
seven, my parents set out a plate of cookies and a glass full
of milk on the dining room table so that Santa would have
a happy snack after climbing down the chimney. On
Christmas Day morning, the plate and the glass stood

empty, which made me an instant believer in Santa Claus.

Then another Christmas Eve soon thereafter, I heard my parents stirring about the house during the wee hours of the night, placing gifts beneath the tree, some of which contained notes in my mother's handwriting, saying "From Santa." It was at that point that I realized I would no longer need to sit in Santa's lap in the department store in order to tell Santa what I wanted for Christmas. For I knew he would no longer be coming down the chimney.

Many moons, Yuletide feasts, and discarded Christmas trees later, I thought to myself, well, gee, wouldn't it be lovely if for just one Christmas we did away with the tinsel, the blinking lights, the fake snow on the Christmas tree, skipped the seasonal glitter altogether and leapt into the New Year without benefit of Rudolph the Red-Nosed Reindeer, the spiked eggnog, the mistletoe, and the Christmas "blues." That wouldn't be so bad after all, would it?

Then suddenly one year a different kind of Christmas catalogue arrived in the mail—not from Walmart, not from Lands' End, not from the store for men who hate to shop for socks and underwear by trapsing all over the mall—and not from Santa's workshop at the North Pole.

No, this one—"The Most Important Gift Catalogue in the World"—came from Heifer International.

For $120 you could give "a dairy goat" that "can supply a family with up to several quarts of nutritious milk a day—a ton of milk a year."

For $20 you could provide a "flock of chicks for families from Cameroon to the Caribbean and add nourishing, life-sustaining eggs to their inadequate diets."

To fight world hunger, a congregation could give a $5,000 "Gift Ark" as a mission project, including "2 Cows to bring milk and income to a Russian village, 2 Oxen to pull plows and carts in Kenya, 2 Sheep to help families in New Mexico produce wool, 2 Water Buffalo for Indonesian families to increase rice production, 2 Camels in India to transport agricultural materials, 2 Donkeys to supply draft power for farmers in Tanzania, 2 Trios of Ducks ... 2 Guinea Pigs ... Rabbits ... Flocks of Geese"... and ... and ... and!

How big did you say that "Gift Ark" is, Noah?

In contrast, how much tinsel and how many blinking lights and Tinker Toys and expensively purchased big-screen TV sets beneath how many Christmas trees are there the world over, Santa Claus?

The Heifer catalog featured this: "It was a Sunday when my mother told me we were going to get a goat which would give us milk. It was the best day of my life!" said Beatrice Biira from Uganda.

The goat gave birth to two more goats which were sold for $200, enabling Beatrice and her family to have "a very good house roofed with iron sheets" instead of thatched grass.

Did someone say "Merry Christmas!" to Beatrice and her family?

Was that someone you, Santa Claus? Or, was it you, Jesus?

And what kind of a make-shift hotel did you say you were born in on Christmas Day, Jesus?

And did I hear it correctly when I heard it said that, like my Santa Claus, you were hung on a tree? With tinsel glistening, and lights blinking, and bells ringing?

And for the sake of chickens hatching, cows milking, oxen pulling, sheep grazing, buffalo plowing, camels trudging, donkeys drafting, and ducks, Guinea pigs, rabbits, and geese mating? And fathers farming, mothers suckling, babies drinking, and children singing?

Is that why we go to the trouble to dress up our Christmas trees, Jesus?

And is that how you asked us to celebrate?

16

Easter at Christmas

"Loveliest of trees, the cherry now
Is hung with bloom along the bough,
And stands about the woodland ride
Wearing white for Eastertide."

—A. E. Housman (1859–1936), "Loveliest of Trees"

OUR LORD JESUS CHRIST KNEW both the best and the worst of human experience. As for the best, he joyously broke bread and poured wine with those who saw in him the promise of God's grace lavished upon all precious children of God whom the world has neglected and rejected at the centers of power and the concentrations of wealth. He extended the very best he had to offer—the certainty of God's kingdom to the least and the lost. He said, "Blessed are you."

As for the worst, our Lord bore the world's evil, guilt, shame, bad manners, greed and violence, upon his own neck and shoulders. He carried his cross to the Place of the Skull where he died an ignominious death, just as other countless, unnamed suffering souls have perished through the ages.

And then he, who was born the meekest of the meek in a lowly manger, broke the bonds of death and removed the shackles of sin. He lifted the eternal darkness by virtue of the fact that the power of God's goodness was at work through him. This is the "gospel"—the "good news"—that

Christmas is never Christmas apart from Easter, else the Christmas nativity long ago would have been forgotten.

The import of Christmas resides not in tinsel and mistletoe, not in gifts placed beneath the Yule tree, and certainly not in the wonderfully popular, pagan myth of Santa Claus, but in the empty tomb of Easter morn.

Had the tomb of Jesus not been emptied and the living Lord not risen, then you and I, and all people everywhere, would die to life, enshrouded in darkness and without the hope that has been revealed in him.

As it is, "the worst of times" turns out to be "the best of times," and the best never finally the worst. This is reason enough to exclaim "Merry Christmas!" For the Christ Event is singularly the merriest of all human events because of what took place at Easter.

In the midst of the world's momentary darkness, the creation groaning in travail, there burns the light eternal of God's ceaseless love, from which nothing can separate us.

"And I, when I am lifted up from the earth, will draw all people to myself" (John 12:32).

Remember this when you postmark your Christmas gifts and trim your Christmas tree. Remember that the infant babe of Bethlehem, the "Man of Sorrows" who "bore our grief" and "was wounded for our transgressions" is the same one whom God raised from the dead.

The meaning of Christmas is revealed in Easter encounter.

He is alive.

And so are we, in him.

PART THREE | Occasions

17

A Day for True Love

"Love's not Time's fool, though rosy lips and cheeks

Within his bending sickle's compass come;

Love alters not with his brief hours and weeks,

But bears it out even to the edge of doom."

—William Shakespeare (1564–1616), "Sonnet 116"

YOU MIGHT SAY that at its inception Saint Valentine's Day was born of the order of a lover's "blizzard." For as legend has it, Saint Valentine, a third century Christian priest, selflessly ministered to his fellow Christians during the storm of persecution instigated by the Roman emperor Claudius. He did so by deliberately defying the emperor's summons for more soldiers to fight his wars. Saint Valentine, brooking no enamorment of imperial power, proceeded to marry young lovers so that the newly-wed husbands could remain home with their wives instead of marching off to battle.

As the legend goes, the gracious and lovingly kind Valentine was met by the wrath of the emperor's henchmen who ceremoniously beheaded the priest on the 14th of February. From this act of ultimate sacrifice, Valentine became known as the revered patron saint of lovers far and wide. During the subsequent annual commemorations of his holy feast day, it was said that the birds of the air joyfully sang their songs of seasonal mating. Thus "The Day of Wine and Roses," now dedicated to the romancing of the hearts of lovers, was granted its nativity in the fire and ice of martyrdom.

As the liturgical season of Lent ushers in its deep consciousness of human sin and suffering, with Ash Wednesday's imposition of ashes culminating in Good Friday's draping of the cross in black, the Christian calendar traces yet another straight line back through time, from the unsaintly decapitation of Saint Valentine to the gruesome cruciform hanging of Jesus of Nazareth. The secular mind, if it notices at all, may deem these two events to possess little more than a remote likeness, a confluence of historical similarities that by now have morphed unrecognizably into the marketable flavor of Godiva chocolates presented with a glass of Champaign wine and a dozen red roses, all very sweet to the scent and taste of postmodern love.

Yet, for the cognizant Christian, with respect to the ancient martyrdom that first took place as a solemn oblation before God, commemorated as Valentine's Day, such an inauspicious "Saint's Day" was not to be the *un*expected consequence of the bloody sacrifice that preceded it on Good Friday.

In both instances human slaughter was exacted at the brutal behest of imperial power. It was concerning just such things that Jesus called his followers to a different way of life: "You know that among the Gentiles those whom they recognize as their rulers lord it over them, and their great ones are tyrants over them. But it is not so among you" (Mark 10:42).

This is not to say that February's "Day of Wine and Roses" should consist of anything less than the most amorous of glorious celebrations, with rosebuds in hand and grapes of affection adorning the lips.

But it is to say that a Hallmark card does not begin to tell the whole story. February the 14th, as we have come to know it, is little more than a gloved hand resting upon a slender shoulder, in contrast to the heavy hand laid upon the head of Saint Valentine, which for the average lover is still hidden from view of the camera.

So, how would it be if we who are Christians were to commemorate February the 14th as a day for true love in the same spirit that Saint Valentine celebrated his defiance of Emperor Claudius in front of the lovers who stood before him, consummated as a martyr's marriage of fire and ice?

What if true lovers everywhere were to join hands and hearts in resistance to imperial edicts that make not for love but for tyranny and war?

How might this change the picture on little red Valentine's Day cards laced with white cutouts, presented with tiny pink, heart-shaped candies, soliciting "Be My Valentine"? The reliquary remains at the shrine of Saint Valentine offer a sobering clue.

When self-absorbed autocrats induce the flame and smoke of repression and war, then the taste of lovers' profoundly sacrificial love, which is true to God's ways rather than Caesar's hunger for power and conquest, is anything but sweet bliss. When this is so, Caesar invariably takes note and refuses to take a backseat to anyone, including God Friday's God and Easter's free Spirit.

True love always defies the unloving ways of bullies and tyrants preying upon the lives and liberties of common folk whose sacred vows to one another make them the true saints.

18

How Beautiful upon the Mountains

I will lift up mine eyes unto the hills, from whence cometh my help. My help cometh from the Lord, which made heaven and earth. —Psalm 121:1–2, KJV

How beautiful upon the mountains are the feet of him that bringeth good tidings, that publisheth peace; that bringeth good tidings of good, that publisheth salvation; that saith unto Zion, Thy God reigneth! —Isaiah 52:7, KJV

GOING BAREFOOT is a lasting temptation. In a child's hop-skip-and-jump world, even in an adult's, being out of shoe has its rewards. The freedom of removing the leather welcomes the pleasure of feeling the grass between the toes. Yet feet exposed to the elements are subject inevitably to the law of cuts and bruises. I remember on several occasions jubilantly chasing the sidewalk in front of my grandparents' house and stubbing my toes on the raised concrete.

Quite early in life, however, I discovered that I did not necessarily stumble any less nor travel any truer for having worn out several pairs of shoes. At the somewhat vulnerable age of thirteen I was scurrying about at summer camp in sneakers one night, in a mighty rush to make it to a movie for which I was late, when in an effort to miss nothing, I took the shortcut behind the movie house. With my weight planted firmly upon one foot, I drove a rusty nail all the way through, from flesh to bone. Let's just say that the deeper wound was the eventual realization that it is possible in this life to step in the *wrong* place at the most hopeful of times. We are never so vulnerable as when we think we are not.

Is it not the *other* person who rivets flesh with the self's stupidity? The *stranger* who succumbs to cancer? The poor children of *foreign* lands who, possessing no shoes, bloody their insides against disease and hunger? Or is there still another order of disease, another dimension of hunger?

* * *

It was near the end of a pleasant week's vacation in the mountains when our seven-month-old and I took a father-daughter stroll, she with her shoes off, and I in tennis shoes laced up with frayed shoestrings. To leap over the image, I was momentarily conscious of being at the *foot* of the mountains, surrounded as it were by the glorious heights and comfort of seeming to be in the *right* place at the most hopeful of times. Even the temperature stood exactly where God willed it at 75°, and the sky Carolina blue.

For the previous six days and without volcanic eruption, those venerable hills had swelled with the song of nine hundred Presbyterians during the annual conference on worship and music. On the seventh day, a planetary silence fell upon Montreat and the handful of us who remained. To borrow a bird's-eye view of the exodus, it appeared as though suddenly an entire ant world, which does most things decently and in order, had retreated from the arched ridges of timber toward the centers of sprawling urban congestion, hairbrained and foolhardy, engines racing, tires spinning, with the zeal of the Lord of Hosts, all, to be sure, to the greater glory of Knox and Calvin, and to fulfill the ancient law of spiritual gravitation which is that all things that go up must come down.

I was fortunate to be among the remnant who were still "up" for at least one more day before having to come "down" to lining up in traffic jams through downtown

Atlanta and competing for a mothball existence amid the city's Babylonian towers of glistening steel and glass. How marvelous "upon the foot of the mountains" to contemplate the peace and poetry of *God's* creation, I thought. If God had wished the mountains to look like Coca-Cola, Georgia Pacific, and the Peachtree Center, the Lord surely would have created them so on the third day.

I had promised myself all week long I would go hear so-and-so preach and congregate with the joyful noise of the nine hundred for upliftance, since seldom does one find in one place so many of the Presbyterian faithful doing quite so much in harmony and unison even if it be nothing more than restrained song. Yet I resisted and chose instead the relaxed conversations of friends, baiting fishing hooks for *our* little wiggle-worms, and quite simply, the mountains.

Katie, our seven-month-old who was entering the wonder-full rite of curiosity, and I, whose passages through this life had not yet, thank God, taken me beyond the need for curious wonder, circled together in the general direction of the general store which at Montreat is more or less at the center of things. I have not figured out precisely where that center is, though I suppose the economic center, at least, would not be far removed from the places in which good Calvinists can lay up their treasures on earth where neither moth nor rust can consume nor thieves break in.

In contrast to the usual twenty to thirty heirs-of-the-covenant lining up between workshops and loading up on sweets and reaching for copies of the *Charlotte Observer* so as not to be out of touch with the invested world of Israeli troops invading Lebanon and the Iron Lady of Britannia sounding like a third cousin to Winston Churchill four times removed, there we were, two or three of us at most, backsliders, milling about in what at Montreat is the closest thing to a sanctified 7-11.

I noticed one "poor" fellow shifting aimlessly from counter to counter as if looking for something that apparently didn't exist, then at last shrugging his shoulders and settling for something which obviously he didn't need. After all, would a conscientious Calvinist have wanted to leave the impression that the "trickle-down" theory of economics did not apply equally to him as he bought a package of *Doritos* for two or three times what it was worth, "bagged" not in Mexico City but first in Dallas and second only in Montreat?

I asked myself, "What must I do to merit my existence in such a world as this?" With no sermon to preach, no pastoral calls to make, not even a copy of Karl Barth's *Römerbrief* to hold up in one hand with a newspaper in the other (of which there was none left since it, too, had been "sold out"), what was I to do? I swiftly purchased a carton of sweet chocolate milk with an expiration date of June twelfth. Does one need a newspaper to tell that the Twelfth Hour approacheth?

* * *

As I sipped, I tasted memories. First, the picture of school days. I recalled how in a state of gathered semi-innocence we coat-and-tie urchins, who never were gathered wholly in any sort of innocence, descended upon the green, nibbled away at cheese crackers, and chased the peanut-butter from the roofs of our mouths with a swish and a gulp of, you guessed it, sweet chocolate milk. The milk was always far more delectable than Mr. M's math class or four-legged sprints during football practice.

So there I stood twenty some odd years later, sipping memories and wondering if I could justify my momentary existence any better by blending the purchase of cheese crackers with the delightful nostalgia of sweet chocolate milk. Shouldn't some things remain always the same? Yet again, I resisted. It was not that I didn't want the cheese crackers, or the preaching, or the congregating in song, but that I was on the verge of the rediscovery of that *other* order of dis-ease, that *other* dimension of hunger, for which the remembrance of things past, events and people, became the catalyst.

My daughter fell asleep in the stroller. My wife and son were off to the nearest village, shopping for Father's Day, and our good friends, as much I fear at risk to our friendship as for renewal of it for having spent the week with us under the same roof, were taking shelter in the laundromat and bemoaning, I'm sure, that the ritual of cleansing is never so much fun as the joy of getting things dirty.

* * *

Katie and I pressed on in our wayward journey behind the general store as years ago I had taken the wayward course through debris to the rear of a movie house, only this time seeking an undefined destination with much less haste than the sum total of destinations I was accustomed to pursuing, and perhaps therefore with considerably less waste, which may be the only way any of us step into the *right* place at the best, the worst, or the most ambiguous of times. There dawns upon us that *all* time is God's time long before it is ours, thus how we embrace it determines how we step into it.

We paused for a moment upon a bridge, one of those *given* moments that is both fleeting and eternal. A bridge can be a grace period. From its slight elevation we got a savoring of the rush and the rapture of a stream that gurgled beneath our feet. Or was it a salient view of ourselves? Are not we Presbyterians, though not uniquely, preoccupied more with the rush of life than with the rapture of life?

102

As one mental association invariably leads to another, I pictured there from the bridge a man who once had sat in my study and asked the timely question: "Have you ever experienced the Rapture?" Choking on my theology, I said, "Do you mean *the* rapture?" When emphatically he said "Yes," as though what else in holy creation could he have been talking about, I quickly answered "No." Then he proceeded to lecture me on the subject, not so much *about* the rapture as *of* it, as though somehow he himself were in it at the time of his telling. I distinctly remember trying not to let go of my critical disbelief; in vain, however. For the only way I could listen to his story was to peel off my shoes, if you know what I mean. Amid all his craziness (and it was!) as he related the deep hurt of his life (the nails!), growing out of years of growing up, or down, during endless nights spent on abandoned street corners and far too many days lost pointlessly taking aim with the barrel of a gun as his only defense against a violent world (a gun which at last be discarded), who the heck was I in all my sanity (and it was!) to deny myself the courtesy of participating with him in the rapture?

* * *

It was then alongside the stream that I noticed Katie awakening to a sound and a sight that in some measure would remain the enduring measure of her days upon the earth through all her growing up and growing down: *the flow of a stream.* She was transfixed! And so was I by her transfixion. She leaned forward as far as the worldly restraint of her seatbelt would allow, inquiring insistently into the first of many overtures of the onsetting events of her life: the rapture of a mountain creek, pristine, crystal clear, unspoiled; that is, almost.

With the constant rippling of those cool waters heating up my imagination, I posed it this way: When you, Katie, pass through these rapids, as do we all, with the downward

103

movement of the current sometimes pulling you faster than you can possibly keep up, then again holding you back when your own sense of timing is delightfully out of sync with the way things are running around you, will it not be the *flow* of your life that matters? Among the rocks, dinosaur, minuscule, slick, jagged rocks that compose the bed upon which a stream must lie, can you not imagine the rudeness of your awakening one day utterly, consciously barefoot in such a world? Or is it the tender joy?

The sum, the measure, the flow of one's life, from whatever vantage point we stand in space and time upon the stream (or sidewalk for urbanites), is that the rush and the rapture are inseparable. Nor do we see for sure from whence they come and whither they go, except when occasionally "to see" from such bridges is to meet the Impenetrable Mystery, the Unfathomable Depth, that, like lofty mountains and great oceans, awaits every pitter-patter, every teardrop, every sound of the rush and the fury which induce troubled breasts to the knowledge that, though we pass this way but once, the Stream is passing forever before us, beyond us, unspeakably beckoning us to take the plunge.

* * *

I just happened to be standing with half a chocolate milk in hand upon soil where Presbyterians had stood "through the ages," seeking refuge *in* these hills, looking for visions *from* these hills. Two collie dogs frolicked in the stream more carefree than the day they were born. I thought to myself, how lucky it is they, not I, who twist ankles in these icy springs, over stones, upon events and circumstances in which animals are made mere participants in the game with such small say as to the inherent dangers and unexpected surprises that await their adventure. They, and not I?

At all points we must choose. For the brook settles and branches in several directions slightly below the bridge. Its friendly passages penetrate a modest park laden with limbs and sliding boards and swings and other such climbing things which give pleasure to the hearts of children, even children who think they are too old to go barefoot in open spaces, yet nonetheless appreciate the ultimate meaning of shoes dropped beneath shade trees on blustery warm afternoons, and the pleasure mixed with the pain of sliding down the very things one must climb up again.

A watchful grandfather sits upon a bench in an obscure corner of the park, glancing widely over his flock of grandchildren who are skipping stones across the surface of things to the splash of laughter, the two collie dogs continuing their sunlit dance, one of them submerging its head beneath a shallow pond and rising again with a pink rubber ball in mouth as though it had at long last retrieved the pearl of great price. "How beautiful upon the mountains are the feet of him who brings good tidings."

* * *

The entire episode, to be sure, from beginning to end was but an interlude, a short glimpse, a reminder forthcoming of the treasure buried in all events. If a treasure, then one which is unearthed at considerable cost, and once gained, easily lost again in the forgetting, in the seasonal sowings of the soul, which, without replenishment, reap scarce harvest. "I lift up mine eyes unto the hills. From whence cometh my help?" What if, in being cast down, there is a persistent failure to look up? Would one then be fortunate to stumble upon the *feet*?

It is at the *foot* of the mountains that the Psalmist's words cling to the ears and lift the eyes in upward glance: "My help cometh from the Lord who made heaven and earth." Is the eternal secret of the mountains that they tilt the head and turn the heart toward Another?

Pilgrims, such as I, are fortunate to make our pilgrimages with extended, even though seemingly endless, excursions through the city. We have a lover's quarrel with the city. At once we love it and hate it. For the city lacks sufficient good tidings to make for the same peace that these mountains do. Thus I wonder at that grandfather sitting over there benched to his years like Wisdom itself pausing to reflect upon vast experience and vaster need. Maybe he lives in these mountains all the time. Maybe he has his origins at this creek, and the living water is the faithsong for quenching his thirst, and the gurgling brook his exceeding joy at returning thanks for the transcendent glory of the creation *in spite of* what is written, no, *in the midst of* what is written in the *Charlotte Observer.*

Grandfather casts his eye upon the grandchildren because he knows. He knows the risk of skipping stones and stubbing toes. He knows that slime upon the rocks spells slippage with shoes or without. He knows the *rush* all right. But he knows something else. You can tell by the way he sits reposed in the quiet confidence of one who is assured that regardless of where one lives or what one has done or not done, it is possible in this life to drink deeply of the divine parable of ordinary events and people.

* * *

Downing the last of the chocolate milk, I consider it is time now to go. In the general direction toward which all flesh must go, savoring last moments before we nurse them as memories, my eye catches sight beside the still waters of an object I had not seen before. Exactly two years ago in this same park, standing virtually in this same place, I had watched venturesome youth, barefoot youth, making preparations for something immeasurably beautiful upon

106

the foot of the mountains, lifting rocks, smoothing out mortar, reconstructing the flow of the stream as artisans at work on something immeasurably important: generations hosting generations to follow. I had witnessed people of the in-between years making ready for things visible, things tangible, which is what a park is. But they were also making way for something intangible, something invisible, something about which they could not have known, nor did I, nor did anyone else at the time except the Lord God of Hosts and a small circle of family and friends who surely must have had the hunch that what was about to happen was happening in all too untimely a fashion.

At my feet was planted a stone. It had not been there before. And it could have been a stone easily overlooked except for the fact that upon it in bronze was a name inscribed. I had visited many public places and seen many names etched in remembrance of persons I had not known, but here was one I knew. And it was as though the very Unnamable One itself suddenly had stood straight up in front of the rest of my life.

Robert Janney Lake was a classmate in seminary. More than that, a friend, a fellow journeyman in the calling. And I shall never forget that beneath his name were but two simple words, "Beloved Minister," which if I translate correctly mean "Beloved *Servant*." And beneath the tribute, a verse from the sacred page which read, "How beautiful upon the mountains are the feet of him who brings good tidings." Some words say it all.

He, for whom this beautiful park is fittingly named in fulfillment of what it was so unceremoniously prepared for, died of cancer before his feet ever had the chance to wear out his shoes. No need for shoes now. As it were, the stone itself had become the beautiful feet, and the bronze plaque the beautiful message of the prophet of the Lord who stands eternally upon the foot of the mountains and preaches, in the midst of the hills, beside the ever-rolling streams, down the time-eroded valleys, into the crime-ridden cities, across the warring continents, in quest of the final horizon. It was as though the eye were upon the foot and the foot were upon the eye, announcing good tidings, proclaiming peace, speaking the tender mercies of the Lord. Can one for certain stub one's toe, one's life, upon that?

* * *

I was sorely tempted to take off my shoes in the Presence. To my embarrassment, it was the adult in me which prevented me from doing so within the child's shadow of that grandfather who, I'm sure, must have noticed anyway, and with whom, as I passed, I exchanged tidings. I wept privately.

"How beautiful upon the mountains are the *feet* of him"—of anyone—"who brings good tidings, who publishes peace . . . who says to Zion, 'Your God reigns.'"

I made a covenant that day before the Lord. Is it not the same Lord who unto *That Day,* without ceasing, makes covenant with us? "Blessed are the peacemakers, for they shall be called the children of God."

Thoughts come home, as meditations, to a nail upon which I stepped as youth, to the nurse who bound up the wound, to the flow of my life which increasingly becomes more vulnerable to the rush *and* the rapture, to the people I cherish for having cherished me before I knew what it was to love, and to events which like this one, when I least expect them, draw me closer to the Feet of the One from whom all things come, and to whom all things go.

19

Once upon a Dream[19]

Among the mature I speak words of wisdom, though not a
wisdom belonging to this present age or to its governing
powers . . . [but of] God's hidden wisdom, his secret
purpose framed from the very beginning to bring us to our
destined glory . . . things beyond our seeing . . . beyond our
hearing . . . beyond our imagining. —I Cor 2:6–9, REB

YOUR STORY, like mine, begins in an unlikely time, an
unlikely place, and for what may seem an unlikely purpose.
Who would have thought that you and I, such as we are,
would be where we are today, or anywhere, as opposed to
nowhere at all?

Millions upon millions of years ago, as life emerged
upon this planet like the unfolding of a fragile flower, it is
said that had the temperature upon the face of the Earth
risen or fallen by so much as one degree, then you and I
would have had no tales to tell and no stories to remember.
For such is the delicacy of each and every moment in time.

Who knows but that every one of us has arrived at *this*
point by a hair's breadth. And, but for that very hair's
breadth, the whole human drama might have turned out
differently. Think of it this way. You are given but one star-
flickering chance within this vast cosmic stretch of time and
space to "do your thing," as we say. Never again in the
course of a billion years will all of us gather in this place for

---

[19] Baccalaureate Sermon, Episcopal High School, Alexandria, Virginia,
the occasion of Mark Fields Davidson's graduation, June 1, 1990.

this purpose, exactly as we do this evening. And, except for those scanty bits and pieces of our pasts that are half-remembered and half-forgotten, which from time to time we revisit like dog-eared snapshots in an old album, we might wonder if the whole thing wasn't just a dream—a life lived *once upon a dream.*

Maybe our stories embrace dreams that are vital clues to our reality. Yet dreams, like events, are chancy things, will-o'-the-wisp things, that are here today and gone-tomorrow. "Out, out, brief candle!" snapped Macbeth. "Life's but a walking shadow, a poor player that struts and frets his hour upon the stage and then is heard no more."

Do we concur with Macbeth that ours is no more than "a tale told by an idiot, full of sound and fury, signifying nothing?"[20] Why, then, these unlikely stories to begin with? Why such wild, improbable stories that by our deepest intuition seem to signify something far more substantial than nothing?

* * *

Some days—I don't know about you—I awake at dawn and sit on the edge of my bed and wait. I wait for my blood to find its equilibrium in the long haul between my toes and brain. The human body presents a hazardous course for a blood cell to travel. Red-and-white-corpuscle creature that I am, called "human," slightly more intelligent than the ape but no steadier on my feet, at six-thirty o'clock in the morning I lumber across the carpet, round the bedpost, stumble over the dog, and grab hold of the doorjamb as I get up a head of steam and make my way toward the kitchen, where between the first and fourth sips of coffee I open the New *York Times* and find the headline,

---

[20] William Shakespeare, *Macbeth*, Act V, Scene v.

"From Nobody to Somebody: John Baldessari, Artist of Ideas."[21]

It's a story about a Los Angeles artist, a so-called Conceptualist, meaning that from out of his head Baldessari conceived and brought forth one hundred art objects consisting of paintings, films, videotapes, books, and photographic works. One of them was a 1967 photograph of himself, beneath which he placed a one-word caption—"Wrong." Sooner or later, he said, we all discover the unfortunate side of ourselves.

There is yet another Baldessari masterpiece, a 1987 photo-collage[22] that juxtaposes the picture of your everyday supermarket next to a carload of corpses from a Nazi concentration camp. As for its meaning, Baldessari said, "I feel that civilization is a thin veneer, and could collapse any moment."

So what do you suppose keeps it going?

Is it a fluke that our civilized world teeters daily on the brink of collective catastrophe, though miraculously it has not teetered *over* the brink—not yet? Is it a fluke that you and I are here tonight, charged with the responsibilities of being educated in such a world? Is it a fluke that some of you chose to be teachers instead of chimneysweeps, and you wonder some days if you will do any more than rid a few minds of a cobweb or two as you scrape away an insignificant amount of cognitive soot? Is it a fluke if perchance you make it all the way through high school, college, and the graduate school of economics and business administration, and at the other end of the procession have something more to your credit than merely a technical

---

[21] Grace Glueck, "From Nobody to Somebody: John Baldessari, Artist of Ideas," *New York Times*, April 4, 1990.
[22]"Inventory," Glueck, *New York Times*, Apr 4, 1990.

education? Is it a fluke if, God help you, you acquire a *moral* education?

The dictionary defines a fluke as a flattened digenetic trematode—translated, a "worm."

What do you suppose are the odds that you and I might have been born the worm? Within the enormous cosmic swirl of possibilities, how come we are given a chance every day to wake up mysteriously human—so human in fact that ours, after all, may not be "a tale told by an idiot, full of sound and fury, signifying nothing," but, on the contrary, an astounding saga in which, as the prophet says, "old men dream dreams, and . . . young men . . . see visions" (Joel 2:28b, REB)? And what if, in the midst of it all, God is the primary Dreamer?

When I was a college student, I arose daily to the horrendous thought that at 8:30 a.m. I would have to face the physics professor. For me physics was a tale told *to* an idiot, not *by* an idiot. Yet I have a deep suspicion that even God is a physicist at heart for having thought up this remarkable universe, and within it the remarkable *unlikelihood* of you and me, as an act of God's graceful dreaming. Once upon a dream *you* became something. There was a time when you were nothing. But this very moment you are *someone* because you were fashioned by God's dream for you.

* * *

I teach philosophy. At least that's what I tell my students I teach. They are gracious and gullible enough to believe me. Philosophy, I tell them, was an ancient science invented by the Greeks to give rational answers to those irrational questions that keep bugging us—questions that every other science as a child of philosophy has been eager to investigate as well.

112

Philosophy is an arrogant business. We *think* we know, as if knowledge were only a matter of thinking. I am frightened by any discipline that thinks it knows without the shadow of a doubt. Perhaps the greatest scientifically, technologically, and philosophically *moral*, and thus human, issue of our time is not that we know too little, but that we may know too much for our own good.

We know the science of operating everyday supermarkets and the science of operating dystopian concentration camps. We have this awesome nuclear problem on our hands. Witness Hiroshima, Nagasaki, and Chernobyl. We have not proven ourselves to be its masters. We are its slaves. Secretly, deep down, we are petrified, or we ought to be. Without limits imposed upon our uses of knowledge, the continuing human story remains in grave jeopardy.

Am I telling you anything you don't already know? But the question is, what are you and I to do about it?

How much leeway do we have to fool around with Mother Earth? Is it by one degree Fahrenheit or by a thousandth of one degree of stupidity that we shall all be made fools with respect to the Earth's changing climate? To think that the dream of a living, pulsating Earth is not only in God's hands but, heaven help us, in yours and mine!

In 1990, you graduate from Episcopal High when not only cities and nations, but also the entire Earth stands at a crossroads. What are the boundaries of human genius, of human powers, that ought not be transgressed?

The twentieth century may be remembered mostly as that century when the human race at last developed and deployed the technologies with which to get really serious about playing God—constantly tinkering around the edges to stretch the limits of human finitude and eventually destroy every living creature by means of the pernicious desire to dominate, control, and conquer. I wonder if such

113

is the grand legacy that ancient Greek philosophy and modern scientism combined have bequeathed us and our children. Westerners, though by no means alone, seem determined to furnish the latest advances in technology that not only can save life but obliterate it.

It is a gross self-deception to conduct public policy based upon the illusion that we can endlessly expend without ever having to pay for the expenditure, and not only with respect to economic resources but also natural resources, as though life were infinitely re-creatable. Accordingly, we proceed as if we will never run out of topsoil and trees and oxygen and fresh water, and that, no matter how prodigal we are, sweet corn, stout wheat, and green beans will forever put forth new shoots in the tundra of baked clay. But is that so?

We should thank God, then, if this urge for self-destruction is not the predominant impulse born of the human need to dream.

* * *

It's a funny thing. My students don't seem to take philosophy as an elective simply because they need another three hours on their transcripts, or because they are thoroughgoing rationalists bent upon understanding and explaining everything that puzzles them about the world. Rather, it's because from somewhere deep from within themselves they stand in awe before the mystery of this great cosmic drama in which they participate, and about which they so desperately want some clues as to how best to live and behave.

Shall they sing and dance, or weep and mourn? Shall they become caregivers of the Earth, or gravediggers? Are they flecks of dust upon billions of galaxies of cosmic meaninglessness, or is there a purpose beyond even the farthest star, a good and certain dream to which they may hitch their wagons?

Our technology is harnessed to spaceships. Our moral and spiritual values may still be hitched to the horse and buggy, which is some respects may be preferable. But the truth is that, in any age, we are lost without *wisdom*—not wisdom as the ancient Greeks conceived of it as knowledge, but moral wisdom as the Hebrew prophets called for it in terms of God's passion for justice and righteousness.

* * *

Each one of you going off to college or university has an obligation to ask yourself and your professors one, big important question. Someday you must also ask it of your bosses and managers, your co-workers, your neighbors, and your children. *What will you do with the big dream?*

What will you do with the dream that God for light years has had for this tiny, revolving sphere in the universe upon whose stage you and I strut and fret?—From the mountainous heights upon which the acid rains are falling, to the delicate rainforests—the "lungs of the earth"—upon which the axe is falling, raping, pillaging, and plundering? And from the ozone dome with which God saw fit to shield our thin skin against the sun's potent rays, to the subterranean streams of water that flow beneath the Earth's crust, intoxicated by uncountable tons of manufactured pollutants? Have we yet made the connection between the drug culture and the drugging of the Earth itself? From Alaska's oil-sickened beaches to Florida's vanishing Everglades—these are the realities about which "the principalities and powers of this present age" are in deep, deep denial. But are you and I?

I concur with Matthew Fox. He's the Dominican priest whose outspokenness landed him in trouble with the Vatican's hierarchy which silenced him for one year, a sure sign that a prophet is not welcome in his own country. Why is it that even the church sometimes conducts itself like the dictator of a banana republic, seeking to silence one of its valid critics? I believe it's because Matthew Fox's book, *The Coming of the Cosmic Christ,* strikes at the core of our barren moral and spiritual consciousness. Recently, Fox was in Ann Arbor, Michigan, lecturing at the University and at First Methodist Church to standing-room only crowds. He said, "When we no longer have any drinkable water because our underground aquifers are poisoned, then we will at last know that Mother Earth is holy, and that all water is *holy water.*"

It is astonishing, when you think of it, that God in all her light years of dreaming, took such a very big chance with us by making us partners—not just co-creators, but co-redeemers of life on this planet.

* * *

Tomorrow, you seniors will graduate. Your mind will soon turn to "higher" education. But higher toward what purpose? You will embark upon careers. But careers toward what end? You may even be dreaming of the day when you become the parent sitting where your parents sit tonight, and when your children sit where you sit. Will you be glad if they yet have a chance to dream?

You are glad.

You are glad that you have had a chance to dream so yourself. You are glad for the sowing of the seed and the harvesting of the fruit for which you have labored while you were here among your teachers and mentors and classmates and friends. You are glad that in their own ways they tried as best they could to give you the best of what God gave them and thus to send you on your way, saying, "Fare well!"

Fare well in a world that has much need of you. Know that your education is not complete until you have aspired and toiled toward those higher things of which Saint Paul spoke, those things beyond our seeing, beyond our hearing, beyond our imagining, prepared for those who love God. You are adequately prepared to face the world only when you have consciously decided to love the God—and the creation of the God—who from Day One has loved you, as incredible as that may seem.

I have a friend in Detroit, Father Ed Farrell, who wrote a small book with the hilarious title *Free to Be Nothing*. In it he states that "everyone wants to be somebody, something. Few dare to remember that we have come from nothing because too many have a terrible unspoken fear that we may return to nothingness."[23] The idea for his book came to him back in 1979 upon the occasion of a visit by Mother Teresa to his Detroit parish church of Saint Agnes. During her visit Mother Teresa said, "The Word of God became man, poor; your word to God became Jesus, poor. And so this terrible emptiness—deep poverty—and your 'yes' is the beginning of . . . becoming empty. It is not how much we really 'have' to give, but how empty we are, so that we can receive fully in our life and let Him live His life in us."[24]

Hearing her words, one of the Saint Agnes parishioners remarked of Mother Teresa, "Her secret is that *she is free to be nothing. Therefore, God can use her for anything.*"[25]

Saint Paul wrote to the Christians of Corinth: "My friends, think what sort of people you are, whom God has called. Few of you are wise by any human standard, few powerful or of noble birth. Yet, to shame the wise, God has chosen what the world counts folly, and to shame what is

---

[23] Edward J. Farrell, *Free to Be Nothing* (Minnesota: Liturgical Press, 1991), 13.
[24] Farrell, 13–14.
[25] Farrell, 13.

strong, God has chosen what the world counts weakness. He has chosen things without rank or standing in the world, mere nothings, to overthrow the existing order" (I Cor 1:26–28 (REB).

Are you ready for this?

My closest friend, who lives in California, called me recently to tell me that the governor of California asked Mother Teresa what he as governor should do about a heavy decision he had to make, which was whether or not to stay the execution of a violent criminal on death row. What do you suppose Mother Teresa said to him?

She looked into the heart of the governor and asked, "What would *Jesus* do?"

It may well be the most important question you will ever ask, and answer, as you stand before your future.

Once upon a dream—once upon "God's hidden wisdom, his secret purpose framed from the very beginning to bring us to our destined glory" (1 Cor 2:7, REB)—what will you do with your life?

To what holy purpose will you signify your days?

PART FOUR | Sacraments

20

Some Wisdom from Woodchuck

"Batter my heart, three-personed God; for You
As yet but knock, breathe, shine, and seek to mend;
That I may rise, and stand, o'erthrow me, and bend
Your force, to break, blow, burn, and make me new."
—John Donne (1571?–1631), "Holy Sonnets" 14

IT IS TRUE. An oyster would have better concocted this beloved mother-of-pearl than I, the pearl-maker, who is left holding nothing but the encrusted shell of a mollusk. What on Earth, I ask, has happened to the luxurious nacre within? My fond creation, all six pages of it, like pearls on a strand, broke loose this past Sunday morning at precisely eleven-thirty o'clock and scattered asunder in every conceivable direction, I know not which way to the good. O Lord, how humbling for such laudable intention to come to naught.

I'm going quietly. I'm going to take these poor, wretched and wrinkled remains to the garden that I have coined Lost Eden, where in solemn retreat I shall find a plot to give them a decent burial. The spent fruits of my labor will lie fallow amid decaying limbs and decomposing leaves. My preacher's bent is simply to be relieved of the perilous burden of wandering futilely farther down a dead-end path into a spiritual desert. This sermon, at last, is finished. I say therefore, "Unto the mercy of Almighty God, I commend the soul of the departed . . . earth to earth, ashes to ashes, dust to dust, in the sure and certain hope of the resurrection."

* * *

I have come to make it my custom to dispose of all my deceased sermons in rich dark loam. When the proclamation of the preacher holds forth little promise whatsoever, the addition of humus to homiletical word-rot increases the chance of supernal growth. Despite its appearance, humus is holy. It is requisite for regeneration.

"Someday," I mumble to myself aloud, "when I'm suckering tomatoes, if I'm lucky and my eyes don't dim, I'll look beneath these weeds and see fresh words sprouting."

"When you find them, nurture them with the sanctity of profound emotion!" chuckled the woodchuck, wobbling its way out of the bush and into the grass.

I was taken aback by this slovenly creature's sudden display of empathy. I took it to mean, "Laugh now. You will have ample opportunity to cry later."

"Well, you, too, old Wobbles!" I blurted out while pondering the tangle of briars a woodchuck must nibble its way through to earn a day's wage.

"Wood and branch must be to you as paper is to me," I wagered. "We seem to bear our fibers in common. Chew them up, and what you get in return is a mouthful of splinters. I get a wad of pasty mush. I don't know about yours, but my congregation deserves better."

"Yes, true," she retorted. "Yet don't forget that dead words, like dead works, may come to life again. Rejoice when they do, and cart them back to your kitchen table and digest them. Don't neglect good fiber if you ever hope to have any substance to your preaching."

"Thanks, my friend," I chortled. "I'll do as you say."

"And watch out for your shadow, too," she snickered, "especially round about the beastly month of February!"

* * *

Given the peculiar speech to which our "profession" is devoted, and as token of the woodchuck's good faith in the potential for the preacher's words to come to life, I cheerfully elected to name my study the Writing Burrow and my prayer stump the Brooding Bench.

That's right. No more trifling diversions, and no more temptation to unworthy pursuits, like paying the bills, revising the calendar, or rearranging the desktop. Strictly writing when in the Writing Burrow and praying when on the Brooding Bench!

I said to the woodchuck that I must do what the ophthalmologist chirped to my daughter when he sought to focus her attention upon the figure on the wall as he shined a bright light into her eyes.

"Keep your eye on the birdie, dear!"

"And don't tarry long over what you just did to your words with the grubbing hoe either, preacher," exclaimed the woodchuck. "You had to bury the lousy things. It was of divine necessity! So pack them down now and leave your depraved pages to the earthworms. Go back to your burrow and start composing again."

"Oh, what does a woodchuck know about composing?" I coughed back. "I say there, wise one, that the important thing is proof texting! Every whole-witted woodchuck knows that composing a sermon is only one-third of the job. The other two-thirds consist of proof texting."

Before I could even think of a verse to quote in support of my argument, she set forth another homily.

"If the Spirit inspires something new and original, and assigns it for you to speak, like the Spirit so moved Moses and Ruth and Jesus, then you will want to test the Spirit to ascertain that it has declared absolutely nothing that can be construed as contradictory to what the scriptures have already said on the subject. Beware especially of those portions of Holy Writ that contradict other portions."

"By golly, Woodie, you do seem to know that certain proof texts are a mighty necessity for adducing the truth, and others simply a nasty nuisance!"

"Yes, for example," she replied, "you must never say, 'You have heard it said, but, lo, I say unto you!' That would be tampering with the most sacred portions of the Holy Book, not to mention the pearls of human tradition."

* * *

Woodie Chuck, as I sometimes affectionately call her, taught me precisely how to refine the retail art of proof texting, that is to say, how to foolproof my sermon for public consumption by settling a weighty theological matter once and forever with all of the authority granted me on Earth as it is in Heaven.

Here's how I do it. I set myself down *elsewhere* than on the bumpy tree stump that is my Brooding Bench to beatify my monkish posture for prayer. And I *avoid* taking my ease in the hardback rocker in the Writing Burrow to puritanize my worldly thought.

What I do, instead, is to stretch myself out horizontally in a comfortable La-Z-Boy next to a roaring hot fire in a dimly lit room, preferably with the received text of His Majesty, King James (whom I'm told is still considered by some to be the long-lost brother of Jesus) open upon my lap.

The poesy of the king, if not the flaming fire at my feet, will surely inveigh against any flimsy interpretation that may unwittingly arise from my own mythological invention.

With proper proof texting as the easy-chair method of solving difficult theological problems without having to bother with the quarrelsome linguistic and contextual details, my sermons shall demonstrate incontrovertibly that God has chosen me to unveil, in instant zealotry, everything concealed that is waiting to be revealed to all who don't yet know anything about it. And, that includes a direct word to every Aunt Gertie and Uncle Gusty who, given their lukewarm piety, or none at all, need to know finally how to "get" themselves saved.

But rest assured it will never be "gotten" by wading verse-by-verse through all the troubling waters churned up by the scandalizing words of Jesus, especially those outlandish things he said about grace abounding in the here and now of God's kingdom.

Who needs abundant grace when certain judgment will do? With the right proof texts at hand we can join forces with Jerry Falwell to erect a modern Masada atop Candler Mountain. There we can hole up as the party of the elect, kill time while waiting for the impending Rapture, avoid the stormy seas of sin and sickness altogether, and shoot arrows at all the infidels who refuse to stand with us.

* * *

Now that my proof texts have been properly lifted from the Bible and placed where they rightfully belong, I move steadily toward completing the sermon.

Rule number one from the Book of Homiletical Proverbs, like rule number one from the Proven Means of Investing, is to "cut your losses."

According to Saint Homileticus, "After you're done mining (please, don't say 'minding') the holy text, and have sufficiently butchered the text to suit your own purposes, you need to wash the sediment out of the sermon."

In that respect, the most proven way I've found to improve my sentences is first of all to stand stark naked in the shower with my manuscript in hand.

To eliminate extraneous theologizing, I do so in the midst of falling water. Not only does the ink disappear miraculously from the page and speedily race down the drain, but as a wet-behind-the-ears theologian, I'm far less likely to catch my socks on fire by proof texting in front of those blazing hot coals in the fireplace, or fall asleep while daydreaming, or allow the sunshine to wrinkle my skin into the leathery look of premature wisdom during a long summer's absence of meaning while lounging about the beach.

Then, with whatever's left for further disposal before I re-write the manuscript, I take a deliberate stroll into Lost Eden. There, with my left hand, I defiantly wield the soaking wet pages and shake them mightily at the sky. Then, with all the strength that I can muster from my right hand while bending over the ground, I plant their soggy remains in the soil from which I proceed to yank up every last weed I can lay my eyes on, lest they find their way into the sermon.

In other words, I "cut my losses" before they begin to take hold of me and the congregation.

* * *

Notwithstanding Jesus's parable about the danger of uprooting the wheat with the tares, I look at Woodie and give her the sum and substance of what all this adds up to.

"Despite my best effort, Woodie, if there should ever be a total lack of wheat in my sermon, then the poor folks

126

in the pew may have no choice but to ingest a bitter weed or two. But what does it matter? A day or so later, they'll recall not a single word of what I said that was worth repeating. Yet they'll remember every last word of what I hoped they'd forget.

"I must admit that the most useless kind of preacher is the one who on Sunday morning cuts a straight line through the middle of the congregation just like a wild, raucous weed-eater going after the thistle.

"Pray tell, what good is any vehicle of salvation, if it kills every single living soul in its path?"

"None whatsoever!" cried Woodie Chuck. "But, rest assured, those dead words, like dead weeds and works, can come to life again after they've found their way to the graveyard. The best sermon, like the best prayer and the best word of advice, is the one born less of repeated shouting than of quiet listening and modest suggestion. The distinction between the former and the latter is the difference between a garden overrun with weeds and a field brimming with wheat."

During my next morning walk around the outskirts of Lost Eden, I overheard Woodie still muttering, "As the wheat grows, the weeds wither."

I replied, "I suppose that means I must do as the good doctor chirped to my daughter. I must keep my eye on the birdie."

Woodie chuckled, "Why, of course, and that's because the birdie knows a thing or two that you don't.

"And take a lesson from me," she said. "Be sure to hold your nose close to the ground and rejoice when those newfound fibers ascend from the 'soil,' precisely where God has hidden them.

"And if you're lucky, you may find the oyster shell and the mother-of-pearl, and even the pearl itself."

21

Of Mites and Miters

"It was too late for man,

But early yet for God;

Creation impotent to help,

But prayer remained our side.

How excellent the heaven,

When earth cannot be had;

How hospitable, then, the face

Of our old neighbor, God!"

—Emily Dickenson, "Time and Eternity" XXXII

MINISTRY IS LIKE SPORTS. It is subject to the pointless competition of the steeplechase, the serious injuries of boxing (with shadows), and the deadly leisure of line drives aimed straight at the preacher, absent the benefit of recreational drugs. Religion alone is dangerous enough as an opiate.

The pastor's life is like the game of golf, minus the combat compensation of seaside, sand dune, and sunshine for duffers in pastel pants and Polo shirts devoting entire careers to sinking itty-bitty balls into trophy-size cups about the size of the average brain.

I've never seen the average poor preacher, with brain, suddenly get converted to being a rich athlete without brain, and I've never seen the average rich athlete, without brain, suddenly get converted to being a poor preacher with brain, after making the first million on the sports field.

So, what does this say about candidates for ordination in the fields of ministry who take the vows of Poverty, Chastity, and Obedience, whether they frame them so or not?

From the start, it's almost guaranteed that at least one of those three hallowed vows-to-do-good will not make it to the finish line. For in the end zone, we meet not only the unfulfilled and once immortal dreams of undaunted youth, but side-by-side with them, the old-beyond-their-years, handicapped, washed-up, wealthy athletes, and yes, the poor preachers, among other creatures with arthritic backs and bunions on their feet.

* * *

At the close of day, God knows not the difference between a poor preacher and a rich athlete, or, for that matter, between rich and poor anything. For, as Jesus said, God "makes his sun rise on the evil and on the good, and sends rain on the just and on the unjust" (Matt 5:45, RSV).

As a pastor and therapist, I have seen rich and poor in roughly equal numbers, though they seldom view themselves as equals. Illusions aside, rich and poor are ultimately afflicted with the same blessings and benefits of Poverty, Chastity, and Obedience that eventually befall us all. Yet it's especially the poor preacher who is supposed to know that those three earthly bonds are what you will "take with you" when your turn comes to "shuffle off this mortal coil." So, why put off until tomorrow what you can enjoy today?

For the sake of your vocation, take your end-of-life vows now. Do so with the best of intentions and good will. Become ordained to subsidiary things like Sunday sermons and bedside prayers since those who habitually chase footballs, baseballs, golf balls, and race cars, are more than glad to leave the incidental stuff to humble preachers while they, the super stars, attend to the World Series and the Super Bowl.

Keep the faith that your routine sermons and cloistered prayers, while promised no earthly reward for luring sports celebrities and big-league players away from life's feigned center of worship known as the winner's circle, will eventually hit "home runs" over the fence that encloses the cemetery, like Babe Ruth swinging all-out for the bleachers.

Remember one thing when you take your solemn oaths. When the "last words" are spoken, it's the poor preacher and not the overpaid athlete who gets to pronounce the benediction at the graveside where Poverty, Chastity, and Obedience *unto death* are eternally ratified.

So, yes, why put off until tomorrow what you can enjoy today? Take your heavenly vows knowing that pastel pants and Polo shirts are about as flattering to a corpse in a casket as steroids are to an athlete who breaks all sports records in order to land himself in jail.

Find a church where the steeple overlooks the cemetery. If you catch yourself boxing at shadows, then take a walk in the cemetery. If you catch yourself receiving lumps from ricocheting line drives while others hammer their hearts away at sweeping home runs, then take a walk in the cemetery. If on your days off you catch yourself spending too much time and money chipping and putting life away on the golf course, and watering more than the grass on the "nineteenth" hole, then take a walk in the cemetery.

When all is said and done, poor preachers ask themselves just who, including the preacher, knows or even cares what the score will be on the tenth and eleventh holes of Sand Castle Links. For when you're standing up, or kneeling down, doing a poor preacher's job of preaching or praying, with one eye on the text and the other eye peering out the window, aimed not at the steeple but at the cemetery, you're suddenly aware of the sacred claim of your calling.

* * *

Preacher, go preach, if you believe in the one whose name is *Grace*. Hers is the gentle wind blowing across the faces of the small people jockeying for the fat-cat owners of thoroughbreds, craving ever bigger purses at the race track.

Grace is the one taking the hard knocks for the lightweights bloodied by the heavyweights throwing punches for the Golden Globe Award at the "box" office.

Grace is the fan standing at the gate outside the stadium, taking up the cause of beggars who never get a chance at the "game" of the hard-hitting swingers whose souls atrophy swatting baseballs aimed at multimillion dollar contracts.

Grace is the one seen mingling with the hookers and slicers of the world who play the fairways of life but never make it into the club house because they keep falling into the sand traps.

Think of the busted Barry Bonds staring down at his cracked bat, realizing that he has hit his last, fast pitch on steroids, and that his trophy for the all-time highest number of homers slammed out of the park is destined for the baseball Hall of Shame. *Grace* has something to say to him, too, about Poverty, Chastity, and Obedience.

Momento mori—remember that you die.

There in the cemetery, anybody who ever did anything, or nothing at all, eventually found out what it means to be Poor, Chaste, and Obedient unto death. And that's why poor preachers and sports champs do well to take long walks in the cemetery. At the end of the day, they have those three things in common and nothing else to brag about.

* * *

Preacher, when you preach, aim low. When you pray, remain at a whisper. Keep one eye on the cemetery, and the other on the widow with the mite in her hand. Her name, too, is *Grace*. Her face is the visage of the back-row mourner standing next to the stone slab etched with a simple cross and the first, middle, and last name, the date of birth and the date of death.

Hidden from vanity, veiled in modesty, she is weeping with the tender wind of the Spirit at her back. Her poverty of body exhibits her chastity of soul, and her chastity of soul her obedience unto death. She is well acquainted with the One who gave her the name of Grace to begin with, and remains content with being Grace until her dying day. It has never crossed her mind that she is the least bit poor in anything when she hears others judge her from the standpoint of their riches and pride, which to her are nothing less than a pot full of fool's gold.

With head bowed and eyes pressed shut, Grace knows what's coming. In her frail and feeble hand she holds the key to what's true for her and true for everyone else. For death spares not the fact that the tiniest mite suffers the same destiny as the tallest miter, to be given away or taken away.

Jesus said, "*Seek ye first the Kingdom of God, and his righteousness; and all these things shall be added unto you*" (Matt 6:33, KJV).

Was Jesus not pressing his point?

At the end of the day, what else is there to be added if, by grace abounding, you have already received the gift of the Kingdom that is present to you now?

22

From Blue Mountain Ridges to Desert Sand Concentration Camps With Stops Along the Way

"Methoughts I heard one calling, 'Child!'

And I replied, 'My Lord!'"

—George Herbert (1593–1633), "Easter Wings"

IT WAS THE SUNNY SUNDAY MORNING of June 23rd, 2019, not unlike other days when the sky is painted blue and gentle breezes waft through the cruciform-flowered dogwoods and stalwart-standing oaks of western North Carolina. Nothing was ostensibly different—not the flow of traffic into the parking lot or the flight of songbirds flitting from tree to tree—that is, except for one thing. *There was deep trouble in the land.*

The Sanctuary

During her sermon on the second Lord's Day after Pentecost at New Hope Presbyterian Church of Asheville, Pastor Kim Wells strode past the milepost marking the home stretch on the long Easter road to just where, nobody could say for sure. Where might a sermon series entitled "Peter, Paul, and Mary: Resurrection Tour 2019" eventually take us?

As she noted with a twist of humor, "Our Peter, Paul, and Mary song for the day is 'Leaving on a Jet Plane.'"[26]

The pre-announced sermon topic had already tipped us off to a dubitable aim for the next leg of the journey: "*Paul: Into the Interior Regions.*" Moreover, the focal text as printed in the bulletin set forth an improbable destination: "*While Apollo was in Corinth, Paul passed through the interior regions and came to Ephesus . . .*"

We are not a congregation of racehorses. With a gathering of worshipers composed largely of sixties- and seventies-somethings, with a Methuselah or two—*sentries*—waving their flags from the bushes, how might a preacher stir an army of aging turtles to move off the log and get trekking?

Paul had once written to the Ephesians:

> I have heard of your faith in the Lord Jesus and your love toward all the saints, and for this reason I do not cease to give thanks for you as I remember you in my prayers. I pray that the God of our Lord Jesus Christ, the Father of glory, may give you a spirit of wisdom and revelation as you come to know him, so that, with the eyes of your heart enlightened, you may know what is the hope to which he has called you . . . and what is the immeasurable greatness of his power for us who believe, according to the working of his great power. God put this power to work in Christ when he raised him from the dead and seated him at his right hand in the heavenly places, far above all rule and authority and power and dominion, not only in this age but also in the age to come. (Eph 1:15–21)

---

[26] Kimberleigh Wells, "Paul: Into the Interior Regions," a sermon, New Hope Presbyterian Church, Asheville, North Carolina (June 23, 2019). Excerpts from the sermon used with her permission.

What if Christ were to put his power to work in us?—we who "were dead through the trespasses and sins in which" we "once lived, following the course of this world, following the ruler of the power of the air, the spirit that is now at work among those who are disobedient" (Eph 2:1–2).

Would it take a brass bell striking like flint to throw enough "spark" in all directions to get things rolling?

The Pastor's Study

Among the myriad of solitary hours the preacher spends within the silent sanctum of her study, pondering the sacred texts of scripture, she listens, she asks, she wonders, she waits, and sometimes broods, to hear the voice of God.

Possessing a meditative heart channeling the Spirit, she practices the contemplative life for spiritual direction. Reflective retreat is not only for refuge in the reigning darkness; it is for being broken open to the approaching light of day.

So, to what possible end might the heavenly hosts be summoning God's people to the Lord-of-Light's present-day calling?

To be sure, the opening sentence of the nineteenth chapter of the Lucan book of Acts is unlikely to set off a shower of fireworks for the preacher or for anyone else. Yet, for a mysterious reason its words stopped Kim Wells *alive* in her tracks. Perhaps because Luke, their author, had something specific in mind to say. And not only Luke, but the Spirit of the Living One who can lift a text straight off the page and placard it squarely in front of your eyes.

"While Apollos was in Corinth, Paul passed through the interior regions and came to Ephesus, where he found some disciples" (Acts 19:1).

If we, the listeners, had wished to obtain the sights and sounds of that screeching, screaming city of Ephesus with its ghettoes, ghouls, goblins, and gibberish, how might we have prepared for the journey through the "interior regions" of Asia Minor?

Completing the reading of the first seven verses, Pastor Kim closed the book of Acts, paused, and spoke.

"So, my question for you this morning is . . . What if we just stopped after preparing? What if we just stopped after preparing without actually doing whatever it was that we were preparing for?"

Cough.

Clear the throat.

Swallow.

"Twelve years ago," she explained,

I took a two-week backpacking course in Alaska. On the first day of the course, we prepared for our backpacking trip by learning how to pack our packs. We went to a park in Fairbanks and spread out all our stuff underneath a large pavilion. Then we learned how to distribute the weight of all that stuff in our packs not only vertically within the pack, but also from the small of your back outwards. We learned how to stuff our packs tightly and make sure that every last air pocket was used. And we learned how to pack in the order in which we would need things—our tents and sleeping bags at the very bottom, since we wouldn't need those until the end of the day, and things like snacks and handkerchiefs and rain jackets would be easily accessible so that we could pull them out quickly.

Yes, yes . . . we're listening now . . . and we're watching.

So, once we had packed our packs and then exploded our packs and repacked them again until we

137

had gotten comfortable with the process, we were finally ready to go back-packing. We got into a van and drove farther north, farther and farther north, way up into the Arctic Circle, until we got to Alaska's northernmost mountain range, called the Brooks Range.

Eventually the van pulled over by the side of the road, and our sense of anticipation heightened. We got out of the van and put those packs on, and then we left the side of the road behind, and without any trail to guide us forward, we simply turned in—into the interior, into the Alaskan wilderness. Over the next two weeks, we backpacked through all the contours of that wilderness, through tundra that was teeming with ripe blueberries. We hiked up huge mountains and along their ridge tops, we looked down on sweeping river valleys, we slept on dry river beds in the light of the Alaskan midnight sunshine, we clambered over boulder fields, we crossed rivers in I-formation knee deep in the rushing water, we fished for Alaskan trout that we cooked over the fire and ate fresh right then and there, we saw caribou and moose and even a few bears from a distance, and we watched the flora and fauna turn from the shades of summer to the shades of fall

But what if we had just stopped after preparing? If we had just stopped after learning how to pack our packs? What if we had spent all that time in the pavilion at the park in Fairbanks and then just said, "Wow, that was great. See ya! Got to get back to the airport!"

Peter, Paul, and Mary—"leaving on a jet plane"—are they?

"What if we spent all that time preparing but then never went on the journey we'd been preparing for? Well, I can tell you that one of the consequences would have been that I never would have had two of the most amazing weeks of my entire life."

Ephesus

Paul had arrived in the city of Ephesus, the seat of the Great Temple of Artemis, the moon goddess and protector of women.

Finding there "a number of converts," he asked, "Did you receive the Holy Spirit when you became believers?"

"They replied, 'No, we have not even heard that there is a Holy Spirit.'"

"Into what then were you baptized?"

"Into John's baptism," they said (Acts 19:2–3).

Must Paul explain that John's baptism was with the water of repentance in preparation for Jesus, the one who came after him, whose sandals John deemed himself unworthy to untie? . . . and that John's converts would now be baptized in Jesus's name and receive the Holy Spirit in order to *speak in tongues and prophesy*? For Luke, to speak in tongues was to make prophetic utterances in more than one language.

There was in Israel—like a rat trap tucked behind a dog bone—a Deuteronomic "sandal-strap" law that said, should a man be unwilling to fulfill the obligation to marry the widow of his deceased brother, then the man should be summoned before "the elders of the town" who were to put the question to him: Will you marry her, or will you not?

If he says, "I have no desire to marry her," then the widow—who otherwise would remain penniless since the money followed the patriarchal line of descent—yes, the widow "shall go up to him in the presence of the elders, pull his sandal off his foot, spit in his face, and declare, 'This is what is done to the man who does not build up his brother's house"' (Deut 25:8–9).

For John the Baptist—whose head was soon to be gruesomely served up on a platter to King Herod—what would it have meant to unloose the thongs of Jesus's sandals?

To disparage him? Repudiate him? Abandon him? Mock him? Spit in his face?

Instead, John baptized Jesus in the River Jordan—that same body of holy water into which Joshua and the twelve tribes of Israel had stepped in order to cross over into the Promised Land, after all those tortuous years of baking and bemoaning in bondage, first as slaves kowtowing to the Pharaoh with his sleazy fleshpots in the interior regions of Egypt, and for forty more years of cold nights and the blazing hot sun in the wilderness sands of the Sinai.

Baptismal Waters

Sunday Baptism in many a reputable churchly tradition has evolved like slow-growing moss on a stone in the forest. It has become the routine ritual blessing of newborns as well as teenage adults and sometimes adult teenagers, by pouring the water, repeating the words, signing the cross, offering the blessing, saying the prayer, lifting the infant mid-air, smiling while the baby "coos," releasing ripples of laughter, snapping a photo of the adoring parents and frowning older siblings, and returning to our seats.

Come Monday morning, we go back to doing what we were doing exactly the way we were doing it last Friday afternoon and Saturday night.

The apostle Paul wrote in his letter "to the saints and faithful brothers and sisters in Colossae," saying of their baptism into the Way of the Crucified One, "when you were buried with him in baptism, you were also raised with him through faith in the power of God, who raised him from the dead. And when you were dead in trespasses . . . God made you alive together with him, when he forgave us all our trespasses, erasing the record that stood against us with its legal demands. He disarmed the rulers and authorities and made a public example of them, triumphing over them in it" (Col 2:12–15).

Jesus had bluntly asked his apostles James and John (yet another John), the sons of Zebedee, the hard question: "Are you able to drink the cup that I drink, or be baptized with the baptism with which I am baptized" (Mark 10:30)?

By repeating in the Gospel of Luke the words of John the Baptist, Luke reiterated what the Baptist had said to his own disciples: "I baptize you with water; but the one who is more powerful than I is coming . . . He will baptize you with the Holy Spirit and fire" (3:16).

Fire?

"It seems," said Pastor Kim, speaking of John's converts, "that their journey had been stopped as soon as they had prepared for it."

Prepared for what? *Fire?*

John had baptized with the waters of repentance. Defining "repentance"—*metanoia*—by its Greek New Testament meaning has the potential to become a revolutionary act. As Pastor Kim noted, it translates "to turn around."

She added, "Turning away from the things in our lives that cause us and others harm and turning toward the God who longs to heal us from that harm and to restore us" is what the word "repentance" is all about.

Not, she concluded, "not that initial repentance, that initial turning back to God as a conversion experience, and that once that conversion has happened, that's all there is to it. Home free! My pack is packed! Time to kick back in the pavilion!"

It is only when Christ's people receive their "fire-power" from the Holy Spirit that the mere thought of being "fired-upon" by the principalities and powers is no longer a *disincentive* to discipleship. Lacking fire from the Spirit, we are already *dead* in our tracks. For there is no incentive to leave the safety and comfort of the pavilion.

The Landing Strip

"Pavilion" Christianity's footprint in the world is comparable to being parked in the yellow "instrumental landing strip critical area" of an airport's runway when we're set to lift off in a jet plane.

How so? Because we're sitting in the danger zone facing the approaching aircraft.

If we're *stalled* there, it may be because we've started down the wrong runway for having imbibed too many pre-baptismal, pre-resurrection gins and tonics consumed on the rocks of theological constipation.

If consequently, we're about to be hit head-on in the fog of night by a careening Boeing 737 Max 8, then the cost to human life will be astronomical. We will have gained nothing for having lost everything from a misguided, underpowered, and failed post-Easter take-off. Worse still, we will have left the passengers at the other end of the flight-path stranded in the "interior regions" without benefit of apostolic *uplift*.

Risk has its reward but risk-aversion little recompense. Sitting stalled in one of the world's "critical areas" is not exactly what Saint Paul had in mind when he left Jerusalem and headed out on the grueling journey to Ephesus.

For those critical areas of life that meet and greet us from both near and far, nothing short of Gospel power will usher us swiftly into the "interior regions" of the mission field. Whether they be in the capital city of Ephesus or tiny hamlets along the way, we can bet our last denarius that God is calling us to something far more demanding than a month's luxury stay at a thousand-year-old marble villa overlooking the banks of the River Cayster.

Be aware, too, that in both Ephesus and Jerusalem, Caesar's armies move about as an ever-imposing colossus. They march in lock-step and, mounted on horseback, gallop through the streets in a formidable show of power. When you least expect them, they will stop you in your tracks and order you to walk a hefty mile with their burdens on your back. It is then that you may have to make a choice. Either offer to carry their burdens a second mile, or, when they slap you on the left cheek, turn the right cheek in a disarming act of defiance. Left cheeks are made for the smacking, right cheeks for the taking down of empire.

Aegean Spaces

About two generations before Paul arrived on the Ephesian scene, the Romans, having permeated all of Asia Minor, sought to do as all imperialists do: adjudicate local disputes between rival kings and rascally kingdoms.

When Mithridates, the great king of the local kingdom of Pontus, finally got sick and tired of Caesar's messing in his porridge, he set about to accomplish the killing of all Romans within catchment distance. Some 80,000 Roman citizens simultaneously perished within six cities stretching across the entire region, including Ephesus.

The blood bath set off another hundred years of warring madness across the Aegean world. That's when the Latin tongue began its decline as a dead language, for if you were caught speaking it, no doubt, you knew exactly what would happen to you next. When historians later labeled these pogroms the "Asiatic Vespers" (an impious euphemism for reprehensible deeds done by evil people) they whitewashed the truth with propaganda.

It's like naming a concentration camp a "child protection center," where children are forced to care for other children while huddling together in wire cages on concrete floors under glaring lights for weeks on end, with no water for baths and only uncooked frozen foods for snacks, because the "adults" have abdicated the palaces of power.

So, on any given day, including the 23rd of June, 2019, there's plenty of reason to cry as you enter the sanctuary of New Hope Presbyterian Church in Asheville, where you're begging to hear a saving word from the living God.

Rome's Playground

The same was true for those Ephesian disciples who welcomed Paul into their midst. If the truth be known, the pagans roaming about the crime-ridden, poverty-stricken, and power-oppressed streets of Ephesus were no less desirous of the same fruits of the Spirit that Paul declared to be available to the newly baptized.

"Each of us was given grace according to the measure of Christ's gift: Therefore it is said, 'When he ascended on high he made captivity itself a captive'" (Eph 4:7–8).

"Captivity" is a killing word. "Resurrection" and "ascension" are saving words.

Incendiary kings and inflamed emperors, preoccupied as they are with "insurrections" and "dissensions" that, due to their prideful pretensions, promote their vested interests, are fearful when they hear the words "resurrection" and "ascension."

When the Roman tetrarch Herod Antipas, son of Herod the Great, received reports of Jesus's whereabouts in Galilee, Herod immediately suspected that John the Baptist, whom he had recently arrested and beheaded, had suddenly "been raised from the dead."

Political paranoia is a sure and certain form of demon possession. No provincial Roman ruler was spared the distant reach of its tentacles. As for Herod Antipas, he had far less to fear from the Jews and Christians than he did from his own reigning emperor, Caligula, who eventually sent Herod packing off into permanent exile in Gaul.

In contrast to Herod's paranoid obsession, when some of the Pharisees came to Jesus, warning him that Herod was out to kill him, Jesus spoke with his characteristic fearlessness: "Go and tell that fox, 'Behold, I cast out demons and perform cures today and tomorrow, and the third day I finish my course'" (Luke 13:32).

It's the small fries acting like big fries who never seem to get the message that provoking fear by threatening, abusing, and oppressing the vulnerable doesn't save fiefdoms and kingdoms any more than it saves their lords and kings from perishing from the fears underlying their own narcissism and self-possession.

The First Epistle of John, the beloved disciple, professed the only antidote to fear. "There is no fear in love, but perfect love casts out fear; for fear has to do with punishment, and whoever fears has not reached perfection in love" (4:18).

The Amphitheater, Ephesus

On an excursion into the "interior regions" of ancient Ephesus we moderns do well to pass by the ruins of the great Ephesian Amphitheater just off the edge of what in Paul's day was called Harbor Street.

We might be gratified to think that we were not among the company of those Ephesian citizens who, during Paul's stay in the city between the years AD 54 and 56, sat inside the theater chomping on their crisp red apples.

That is to say, we might be glad that we were not among those pavilion people, because things got a bit out of hand when Paul and some of the other Jews and Christians began to stir things up in Ephesus. Although, if we had been present, we might have felt fortunate to be singled out when Paul sauntered over toward us as he made his way through the crowd.

Since pessimism offers no hope where optimism breeds naiveté, what do you think Paul might have said to us situated there in the interior regions of a fallen world, not unlike our own, in the age of the Caesars? Would he have said that there's no need for us resurrection people to go about fretting with frowns on our faces due to all the unsettling events in the city?

Perhaps he would have spoken to us the very words he later wrote to the Christians at Philippi, which he put together from a prison cell in Rome not long before his execution.

> I want you to know, beloved, that what has happened to me has actually helped to spread the gospel, so that it has become known throughout the whole imperial guard and to everyone else that my imprisonment is for Christ; and most of the brothers and sisters, having been made confident in the Lord by my imprisonment, dare to speak the word of God with greater boldness and without fear. (Phil 1:12–14)

> If there is any encouragement in Christ, any consolation from love, any sharing of the Spirit, any compassion and sympathy, make my joy complete: be of the same mind, having the same love, being

in full accord and of one mind. Do nothing from selfish ambition or conceit, but in humility regard others as better than yourselves. Let each of you look not to your own interests, but to the interests of others. Let the same mind be in you that was in Christ Jesus, who, though he was in the form of God, did not regard equality with God as something to be exploited, but emptied himself, taking the form of a slave, being born in human likeness. And being found in human form, he humbled himself and became obedient to the point of death—even death on a cross. (2:1–8)

What do Paul's words of encouragement mean then for us as we, like the Ephesians, gather in our spaces of worship where as Christians we sing hymns and say prayers, hear sermons and celebrate sacraments, during the Lord's Day liturgy?

Surprisingly, the English word "liturgy" is derived from the New Testament Greek word *leitourgia*, which signifies more than the "work" we do in the "service" of worship. *Leitourgia* also denotes the public service, the relief "work," that as Christ's followers we undertake in the world at our own expense.

But what is "expense"?

As our pastor Kim said, the expense may consist of rugged treks through wilderness terrain "over boulder fields" . . . sleeping in "dry river beds" . . . stepping into our boots like "blocks of ice . . . frozen solid in the night," during a sojourn in which "there's nothing like doing a face-plant in the mud when your pack is forty-five percent of your body weight and comes right down . . . on top of you."

As Kim went on to say, because we are resurrection people and not pavilion people, "The Holy Spirit takes us beyond preparing and nudges us out of the van and helps us get our packs on and then takes us *in*—deep into the interior regions of both our inner landscape and God's."

And since the Holy Spirit takes us "beyond" preparing, which is what we do when we worship, and nudges us on and takes us "in," then that's really all we need to know *for sure* during any given moment of the journey.

The "Ice" Wagon

Unlike guests at the local country club ordering Johnnie-on-the-rocks (iced) Scotch, when a Latina mother in the trailer park hears the word "ice," she's not dreaming of leaving for a sightseeing expedition on a cruise ship lapping about the melting ice-caps north of Baffin Bay in the Arctic Circle.

She's having nightmares about the circular handcuffs locked around her husband's wrists in the wee hours of the morning, when ICE knocks on the door and freezes her heart to stone at the sight of deportation papers as she watches her beloved whisked off in front of the children, not to be seen again.

One of Caesar's favorite ploys is to freeze people out when he can't find warmth in his heart to welcome them in. His politics crystalize as ice in his veins.

Contemptuously labeling them "illegals" is Caesar's first measure for deep-freezing them.

Detaining them at length with or without due process is Caesar's second measure for deep-freezing them.

Casting them overboard from the ship of state is Caesar's final measure for deep-freezing them.

Yet, to resurrection people, to Christ's people, the persons whom Caesar's hardened heart deep-freezes as the offscouring of the earth are the very people whom Christ calls his own.

Resurrection people offer them food when they're hungry and drink when they thirst, clothing when they're naked, and visit them when they're sick and in prison.

Resurrection people bear witness to what Jesus declared of the dispossessed: "Truly, I tell you, just as you did it to one of the least of these who are members of my family, you did it to me" (Matt 25:40).

It was in that same spirit of restoration that Paul once wrote to the beloved in Ephesus.

"But now in Christ Jesus you who once were far off have been brought near by the blood of Christ. For he is our peace; in his flesh he has made both groups into one and has broken down the dividing wall, that is, the hostility between us. He has abolished the law with its commandments and ordinances that he might create in himself one new humanity in place of the two" (Eph 2:13-15).

And that's just the trouble with Paul, which—have you noticed?—keeps getting him into trouble. He's always busy breaking down the walls of hostility that divide. He's always got his eyes on the "new humanity" in Christ when the old humanity has failed us.

The Temple of Artemis

The past and present threads of history are closely woven. If city dwellers in ancient Ephesus could have answered the longings of the fainthearted and disinherited among them, to which temple do you suppose they would have pointed them?

Artemis reigned not only as moon goddess and protector of women, but also as deity of the wilderness, the hunt, and wild animals. Her veneration extended far beyond the peripheral bounds of the metropolis. Pilgrims carried to home and hearth the smelted tokens signifying her ostensible powers. Her temple stood as one of the seven wonders of the world. It contained great works of art and throngs of travelers from every corner of the civilized earth came to visit her.

The book of Acts states that pandemonium fell upon Ephesus when "God did extraordinary miracles by the hand of Paul, so that handkerchiefs or aprons were carried away from his body to the sick, and diseases left them and the evil spirits came out of them" (19:11–12).

And, once again, Paul got himself into trouble.

> About that time there arose no little stir concerning the Way. For a man named Demetrius, a silversmith, who made silver shrines of Artemis, brought no little business to the craftsmen. These he gathered together, with the workers of like occupation, and said, "Men, you know that from this business we have our wealth. And you see and hear that not only at Ephesus but almost throughout all Asia this Paul has persuaded and turned away a considerable company of people, saying that gods made with hands are not gods. And there is danger not only that this trade of ours may come into disrepute but also that the temple of the great goddess Artemis will be scorned, and she will be deprived of her majesty that brought all Asia and the world to worship her." (Acts 19:23–27)

So—"When they heard this they were enraged, and cried out, 'Great is Artemis of the Ephesians!'" (19:28).

But then, two hundred and thirty-some years after the life of Jesus, Romans and Greeks across the empire took note of the fact that, due to the ruthless raids and attacks of eastern Germanic peoples called the Goths, the Temple of Queen Artemis was leveled to the ground, never to rise again.

What chance do you suppose there was that Paul and those Jewish and Gentile Christians with whom he aligned himself had something to do with Queen Artemis's demise?

It was, after all, a costly endeavor. Paul did not live to see the fruits of his labor, but he left us an account of the price of his toil.

> Three times I was beaten with rods. Once I received a stoning. Three times I was shipwrecked; for a night and a day I was adrift at sea; on frequent journeys, danger from bandits, danger from my own people, danger from Gentiles, danger in the city, danger in the wilderness, danger at sea, danger from false brothers and sisters; in toil and hardship, through many a sleepless night, hungry and thirsty, often without food, cold and naked. And, besides other things, I am under daily pressure because of my anxiety for all the churches. (2 Cor 11:25–28)

So, what did Paul conclude as to how we resurrection people are to conduct ourselves as a result of Paul's own adversities and endeavors?

"When reviled," he said, "we bless; when persecuted, we endure. When slandered we speak kindly. We have become like the rubbish of the world, the dregs of all things, to this very day" (1 Cor 4:12b–13).

"I appeal to you, then, be imitators of me" (4:16).

Clint, Texas

Unlike Paul, we are "established" Presbyterians. We are aged like softened, cleanly sliced cuts of ripened Dunsyre blue cheese ready for crumbling in Caesar's salad.

We have gathered this morning on the 23rd of June in Asheville. As the faithful sheep we seek to be, we are grazing for holy sustenance beneath the motherly embrace of these Blue Ridge Mountains, visible in all their majestic splendor through the clear glass window that frames the vista beyond the cross and communion table. We can see as far as the Spirit ferries our vision.

Pastor Kim's reading of the scripture and her sermon from Acts have led us, with Paul, into the "interior regions." We are still some miles from the clamor and travail of the city of Ephesus, but we are on our way.

We are soon to receive the benediction after singing the morning's closing hymn: "Spirit, spirit of gentleness. / Blow through the wilderness, calling and free."

For us Presbyterians of the Protestant Reformed tradition, it is a rare thing to have what Pastor Kim calls a "Quaker moment." But on this particular occasion, the "Spirit within" is calling.

Could there ever be a more propitious moment for one of the retired shepherds from within the flock to be moved to speak before the congregation simply because not to speak would be to leave the Spirit churning and breathless among us as we take our leave?

"Friends, dear ones, fellow members of the body of Christ, beloved—

"I have not slept well all this past week. I was awakened by the nightmare of seeing myself barricaded along with these children within the walls and wired cages of that concentration camp in the desert sands of Clint, Texas. You know the story. You've heard and seen the news.

"I simply cannot sit silently any longer. I will not stand idly by.

"I can't tell you when I've been so thoroughly outraged as to what is happening to these dear children in the camp.

"Not enough water. Not enough food. Unsanitary conditions. Barred from medical care. Crowded next to one another in standing room only for weeks on end. Ceiling lights glaring down upon their faces twenty-four hours day and night. Sleeping on concrete. No windows through which to see beyond their perilous plight to plead for help. No one to comfort their cries in the dead of the night or dispel their fears in the fever of day.

"For heaven's sake and for theirs, what are you and I going to do for them?

"Yesterday I contacted the offices of Governor Gregg Abbott of Texas, and Senators Cruz and Cornyn, as well as Governor Cooper of North Carolina. Tomorrow I will be calling others.

"I want to ask you. I want to ask you to do whatever you can. Write. Email. Pick up your phone. Make calls to politicians in Texas and other parts of the land. Make calls to your friends. Make calls to anyone you know who can bring influence to bear upon the situation. Aim as high and far as you possibly can. For until these children receive immediate relief, they remain at grave risk of perishing within the confines of this concentration camp.

"Let's get going. Let's get going together into the 'interior regions.'

"But before Kim offers the benediction, let's bow our heads in silence and prayer for these children—*God's* children—*our* brothers and sisters, *our* sons and daughters in Christ."

   In her benediction, Pastor Kim charged the congregation to go forth and act boldly.

23

Do You See the Faces of the Children at Our Borders?

Addressed to a 2019 public gathering at Calvary Presbyterian Church, Asheville, North Carolina, in response to the families and children detained and caged at the border.

Look, with your compassionate heart, squarely into the faces of these girls and boys being snatched from the longing embrace of their parents and siblings. Give your undistracted concentration to their terrified, disbelieving gazes.

Bear witness to their utter humiliation as they are handcuffed by strangers in armed uniforms and secreted off in unmarked vehicles to undisclosed locations.

Pause yet again, giving your rapt attention to the emotional torture they suffer as they watch their parents being booked as criminals and hauled away to prison.

Observe with deepest empathy their tender youth, incarcerated behind locked doors, barricaded in warehouses behind walls sealed shut with windows blackened, and crammed into wire cages off-limits to parental and public inspection.

Approach them, not from the president's, the attorney general's, or ICE's authoritarian perspective, which is demonstrably antithetical to their personal wellbeing. Rather, let your benevolent mind's eye see them from their own simple, delicate, fragile perspectives. Let your earnest glances grace them as kindly and surely as you would the faces of your very own children.

Imagine yourself as though you were the one confined in their palpable predicament. If by good fortune you are a parent, grandparent, or guardian, then for heaven's sake, for a clear-eyed single minute's sake, for the children's sake, paint the faces of these latch-cage kids into your children's and grandchildren's faces.

Do you grasp their foreboding and fear as the torrents of tears stream down their tender cheeks? Do you catch their feverish eyes searching frantically for familiar faces within these cold, concrete, unfamiliar spaces? Do you notice their arms, hands, fingers—entire bodies—longing to be held within their mothers' and fathers' warm, comforting embraces?

Are you seeing them now?

Are you hearing what in their immediate plight they strain to hear beyond the clamor of their clanking steel encasements? Are you seized by their frenzied screams, their panicked sobs, their morning groans, their midnight whimpers? Do you feel the knots gnawing at their stomachs, the tremors wracking their bones?

Are you listening to them now?

From where they lie panicked and distraught upon cement-hardened floors where once stood shelves lined with teddy bears, little girls' fancy dolls, and little boys' water pistols, is there anyone who can explain what's impossible for them to understand apart from Mommy's and Daddy's consoling hands and arms?

Are you seeing and hearing them now? Are you moving yet?

Is there an interlocutor of sure and certain voice, of undeterred demeanor, willing to stand firm, refusing to take no for an answer, demanding justice where there is no mercy and mercy where there is no justice, calling for the release of God's beloved children from the cold and heartless hand of the oppressor?

Will you speak for them now? Will you move for them now?

"Surely, thus says the Lord: Even the captives of the mighty shall be taken, and the prey of the tyrant be rescued, for I will contend with those who contend with you, and I will save your children" (Isa 49:25).

Is it you, then, whom the prophet summons to contend with the contender?

Is it you who will camp at the doorsteps of legislators until they relinquish the yokes of burden they have placed upon the necks of the sojourner and the backs of the poor?

Is it you who will stand unarmed before the chiefs of police to insist that they extend the hand of genuine friendship to the immigrant terrified by judicial orders, squad cars, uniforms, badges, billy clubs, stun guns, revolvers, and arrest warrants?

Is it you who will intervene in the courts of justice on behalf of those whom the principalities and powers have herded into detention centers and locked into prisoners' dens by the force of their decrees and the stroke of their pens?

Is it you who by the strength and power of God's saving hand will stand boldly before the councils of the mighty to contend for these little ones with loving kindness and deeds of tender mercy?

For it is Jesus who calls them blessèd.

"Let the little children come to me, and do not hinder them; for to such belongs the kingdom of heaven" (Matt 19:14, RSV).

It is we whom he summons and sends.

It is we who stand, and move, and act, and speak together, saying—

"Here am I, O God, send me."

24

Bannocks (Loaves) of Bread

I simply argue that the Cross be raised again at the centre of the market place as well as on the steeple of the church. I am recovering the claim that Jesus was not crucified between two candles, but on a Cross between two thieves; on the town garbage heap; at a crossroad so cosmopolitan that they had to write his title in Hebrew and in Latin and in Greek (or shall we say in English, in Bantu, and in Afrikaans?); at the kind of place where cynics talk smut, and thieves curse, and soldiers gamble. Because that is where He died. And that is what He died about. And that is where church[people] should be and what church[people] should be about.[27]

—George MacLeod, Founder of the Iona Community

IN THE SUMMER OF 1965, I spent a memorable week on the tiny island of Iona off of the west coast of Scotland, the site to which Saint Columba came from Ireland in AD 563, to inaugurate the Christian mission to northern Britain.

Amid the Great Depression in 1938, George MacLeod, a Scottish minister from an industrial section of

---

[27] George F. MacLeod, *Only One Way Left* (Glasgow: The Iona Community, n.d.), 38. The book is derived from lectures that George MacLeod gave at New College, Edinburg, Scotland, and at Union Theological Seminary, New York City, in 1954. He wrote: "Laity who attended the lectures in both countries were in the forefront of the demand that they be incorporated in book form." The general thesis is that "the Christian must be concerned with politics in his role as citizen" (vii).

Glasgow, brought together on the island a half dozen craftsmen and six or so young ministers. They labored with their hands during that summer and subsequent ones to reconstruct the ancient medieval cathedral buildings which had fallen into ruin. Their objective was to establish a common life and discipline of worship and work, of stewardship of time and money, renewing their covenant in Christ in order to return to the cities and factories of the mainland with an expanded vision of their Christian witness, where they continued the discipline.

From that rather inconspicuous beginning, there emerged a global fellowship of laity and clergy who have come to be known as the Iona Community. Their pilgrimages to the island today are for the same purposes as for their predecessors, groups of whom meet in other lands.

My memory of Iona has stuck with me through the years. There I recall my own pilgrimage for its daily morning and evening trek over heath and fence to the beautiful greystone Abbey of Saint Columba. The churchyard is graced with the thousand-year-old Cross of Saint Martin and tombstones commemorating pilgrimages of saints and sinners from earlier times, including the renowned Duncan and Macbeth. One in our group referred to Iona as the paradise where God takes sabbaticals.

The worship that week was among the most compelling I have ever encountered. The liturgies were a blend of a timeless living tradition and a deep sensitivity to the contemporary human condition. Memory preserves even now the simple echoes of sacred sound reverberating from the balcony piano . . . hushed silences beneath the vaulted ceiling between vesper biddings . . . the liturgist's reading of inspired words from an "ambassador in chains" to the Ephesians, with the prayer that the gospel be boldly proclaimed . . . the flux of worshippers presenting bodies and souls for consecration at the midweek service of healing

. . . and the solemn thanksgiving processional of bread and wine to the holy table on the Lord's Day.

These were not all. The *koinonia* of several hundred sojourners had congregated from faraway lands and diverse Christian traditions. Faces were not the same nor accents familiar. It was incumbent upon all to build bridges.

My final recollection consists of the serious nature of theological conversation, in itself a form of prayer, as George MacLeod sat in our midst to speak with us for an hour each morning. Never did the chatter of voices drift from the complex individual, social, economic, and political realities that comprise the framework of every Christian's vocation. There lay before us the real issues of life and death, of discipleship and spiritual formation. Iona was not for escape. That was the summer of rioting in Watts, war in Vietnam, strife in Northern Ireland, and starvation in the Orient. All of those realities were mixed in.

Iona is a spiritual center in a whirling vortex. Geographically removed, it is planted at the heart of a groaning creation, a "thin place" in the eye of the tempest. Steady offshore gusts are reminders.

So, what was gained? Very simply, one thing. An image of the church at the crossroads: worship the centripetal event, mission the centrifugal event. Both are one service, "always carrying in the body the death of Jesus, so that the life of Jesus may also be manifested in our bodies" (2 Cor 4:10).

When visitors to Iona take holy communion, they proceed directly afterward to the cloister for tea and conversation. The concluding rubric of the liturgy states that each worshiper will be given "small bannocks of bread to flake and share" while mingling with strangers. "Thus is communion brought into the ordinary ways of life."

160

Saints, as forgiven sinners, are "bannocks of bread," the loaves of the Christ at the crossroads of a hungry world.

Acknowledgments

I wish to express my personal gratitude to David Russell Tullock, publisher, and Tammy Swiney Reynolds, administrator, of Parson's Porch Books, for their dedication, competence, and kindness in bringing *Foster's Pie Pan* to fruition, as well as to former and current editors of *The Presbyterian Outlook*, *Theology Today*, *Vox Populi: A Public Sphere for Poetry, Politics, and Nature*, and to the staff of the Presbyterian Publishing Corporation, who first published the following chapters which in several instances have been revised for this collection.

* * *

"A Day for True Love." *The Presbyterian Outlook* 184 (February 11, 2002).

"A World of Surprises." *The Presbyterian Outlook* 185 (January 13–20, 2003).

"Bannocks (Loaves) of Bread." *Today's Word for Adults* 3 (Summer 1981) 4.2.

"'Best and Deepest Self-Portraits.'" *Vox Populi: A Public Sphere for Poetry, Politics, and Nature* (October 30, 2022).

"Cry, Advent" (originally "Advent, a Season of Prayer"). *The Presbyterian Outlook* 173 (November 25, 1991).

"Christmas Trees" (originally "Christmas Evermore"). *The Presbyterian Outlook* 184 (December 20, 2002).

"Easter at Christmas." *The Presbyterian Outlook* 184 (December 22, 2003).

"Foster's Pie Pan." *The Presbyterian Outlook* 184 (March 11, 2002).

"From Blue Mountain Ridges to Desert-Sands Concentration Camps." *Vox Populi: A Public Sphere for Poetry, Politics, and Nature* (July 7, 2019).

"Grace Given as Grace Received." *The Presbyterian Outlook* 184 (October 21, 2002).

"How Beautiful upon the Mountains." *Theology Today* XLV (July 1984) 154–160.

"Of Mites and Miters." *The Presbyterian Outlook* 190 (February 11, 2008).

"Portraits of You" (originally "You"). *The Presbyterian Outlook* 184 (September 30, 2002).

"Quiet, Please! While the Fox Is Passing!" *The Presbyterian Outlook* 184 (June 10, 2002).

"Sea Saga." *Vox Populi: A Public Sphere for Poetry, Politics, and Nature* (April 17, 2022).

"Some Wisdom from Woodchuck." *The Presbyterian Outlook* 184 (November 25, 2002).

"The Bitter Frost and the Wild Snowflake." *The Presbyterian Outlook* 183 (December 24, 2002).

"The Slaves of My Ancestors" (originally "The Line of Vision"). *The Presbyterian Outlook* 184 (August 5–12, 2002).

www.ingramcontent.com/pod-product-compliance
Lightning Source LLC
Chambersburg PA
CBHW072045090426
42733CB00032B/2261